Get Your Story Straight

A Step-By-Step Guide to Screenwriting
by a Million-Dollar Screenwriter

by
Diane Drake

To my students, with heartfelt gratitude for their appreciation and encouragement.

Table of Contents

PREFACE

"A word after a word after a word is power."

~ Margaret Atwood

SOMETIMES IT SEEMS AS THOUGH each new screenwriting book on the market, perhaps in an effort to offer some new ground-breaking, sure-fire formula, contains ever more complex graphs and charts and elaborate jargon and theories of writing. These things make my head spin. I become hopelessly mired in trying to even understand the concepts set forth, let alone apply them to my own work. And if they do that to me, somebody who's actually written and sold screenplays and had movies produced, I can only imagine how daunting they must be to writers just starting out.

Having worked as a screenwriter of "major motion pictures," in development as a Vice President of Creative Affairs for Academy Award-winning director/producer Sydney Pollack, as a story consultant, and as a writing instructor for the UCLA Extension Writers Program, I wanted to share what I've learned to help empower other writers. So one of my main goals here is to try not to make matters any more complicated than they already are, because they're already complicated enough.

I've boiled down what I believe are the most essential principles and elements that go into writing a satisfying story and successful screenplay. I've also put a lot of emphasis on story structure, as I think creating a solid one is challenging, yet key to crafting a great script. And since screenwriting is a spare art, I've endeavored to take novelist Elmore Leonard's advice and have done my best to "leave out the parts people skip."

All of that said, I'll be the first to admit that there simply is no single rock-solid formula to this craft. Would that there were! There are principles, but this is art, not math, and one of the big challenges of creating something original is that it's the prototype every time out. On the plus side, you are free to—in fact, I would say you are charged to—create something the world has not yet seen.

And on that note, I salute you. The creative path in life is often not an easy one. It can sometimes feel like the path of most resistance and it takes courage to pursue. But as the Zen proverb tells us, "The obstacles are the path." It is in the process of striving to overcome the challenges in life that we and, not at all incidentally, our fictional heroes, grow.

May you, like any good protagonist, allow the creative and personal challenges in your life to help bring you to a higher realization of yourself. And may this book help encourage you to do that. May it provide you with some useful tools with which to share your own unique voice and vision and, as Tolstoy advised, "Add your light to the sum of light."

INTRODUCTION

> "To make a great film you need three things –
> the script, the script and the script."
>
> ~ Alfred Hitchcock

I HAVE STRUCTURED THIS BOOK TO provide an insider's guide to what it actually takes to get your story straight as a screenwriter. I will take you on this journey from the outside in, first discussing story and movies, then zooming in on the specifics of screenplay construction, and finally describing what it's really like to work in "the" industry.

In the first couple of chapters, I address the larger topics of why we write and what movies are really about. In Chapters Three and Four, I'll take a step closer and describe how to choose a concept, and how to distill a short but pithy "log line" from that concept. Creating a log line is imperative in crafting your story, as it serves as an abbreviated map or spine for your script. It's also a tool required in the business; an intriguing log line can help sell your screenplay.

In Chapter Five, I give you an overview of the classic three-act structure of screenplays: what it is, how it works, and why it's necessary. It's so important that even if you choose to abandon this traditional paradigm of storytelling, you need to understand it before you discard it. As the saying goes, you need to know the rules before you can break them.

In Chapter Five I also begin my analyses of ten screenplays that were each the basis of successful movies. In each chapter thereafter, I use these "Structurally Speaking" sections to illustrate the concepts I cover in the book. I also deconstruct the three acts in each script to expose their working parts. In teaching screenwriting I've found that explaining a concept is great, but demonstrating it in action is even better. I endeavor to show how the same screenwriting concepts and elements are used time and again in different ways in well-known, commercial films. Please refer to the section at the end of this Introduction entitled "Suggested Movies to Watch" for more information.

Starting in Chapter Six and continuing through Chapter Eight, I explore each of the three Acts in greater detail. I cover their specific aims, elements, timing, and how they fit into the larger picture. The diagnostics I provide in these chapters are intended to enable you to create your strongest work possible. They'll serve a roadmap as you write, or a guide as you re-write, and help you pinpoint and correct problems that may stem from issues specific to each Act.

For the following few chapters, I explain how to populate those Acts: with interesting characters, especially heroes (Chapter Nine) and villains (Chapter Ten); with well-structured scenes in Chapter Eleven; and with evocative dialogue that keeps the story moving in Chapter Twelve.

Chapters Thirteen and Fourteen focus on the business. I discuss what you can expect in Tinseltown, how best to try to break in, and how to protect yourself and your work. Finally, in Chapter Fifteen I close with a few words about what it's really like to be a content creator, and how to keep the inspiration flowing.

Stylistically, you'll note that throughout I use the default pronoun "he" whenever referring to characters or writers, something which honestly kind of bothers me. I'd hoped to use the more gender neutral "they" and "their," as I do in my teaching, but my copy editor slapped my wrist for that impropriety and I fell back on traditional "he." I promise to level the playing field and invoke Title IX in my next book.

Finally, you will see that at the end of each chapter I include a summary list of Takeaways as well as a list of thought-provoking questions or exercises to help keep your creative juices flowing. Throughout the book, I've also included links to relevant videos and other websites which accent or illustrate my points. The videos offer advice, insights and humor from some giants in the industry, most of whom have faced the same sorts of challenges you will face as a screenwriter.

In short, I have endeavored to provide you with the kind of book I wish I'd had when I was first starting out as a screenwriter.

SUGGESTED MOVIES TO WATCH:

I'll analyze some of the films listed below in detail; others are referenced more sparingly with regard to particular elements. I've endeavored to mix things up, between new and old; solo hero, buddy picture and ensemble; male and female leads; drama; comedy; animation; indie; superhero; action and thriller. Most are critically and/or popularly successful movies, many of them based on Oscar-winning screenplays. You learn best from the best.

500 DAYS OF SUMMER	PULP FICTION
ARGO*	ROMAN HOLIDAY*
BRIDESMAIDS	SIDEWAYS*
ERIN BROCKOVICH	THE 40-YEAR-OLD VIRGIN*
GOOD WILL HUNTING	THE HANGOVER
IRON MAN*	THE KING'S SPEECH*
IT'S A WONDERFUL LIFE	THE PLAYER
LITTLE MISS SUNSHINE*	THELMA & LOUISE*
LOST IN TRANSLATION	TOOTSIE*
MR. & MRS. SMITH	TOY STORY*
ONLY YOU	WHAT WOMEN WANT

*In-depth script analyses of each of these films are included. I strongly urge you not only to watch these particular movies at least once, but also to read their screenplays, almost all of which are available online. I also encourage you to read the scripts for any films you especially love, as seeing work laid out on the page is essential for anyone who endeavors to write screenplays.

CHAPTER ONE

WHY WRITE?

> *"Who wants to become a writer? And why? Because it's the answer to everything. It's the streaming reason for living. To note, to pin down, to build up, to create, to be astonished at nothing, to cherish the oddities, to let nothing go down the drain, to make something, to make a great flower out of life, even if it's a cactus."*
>
> ~ Enid Bagnold

W E ALL LOVE GOOD STORIES, we crave them from a very early age. I believe it's something deep in our DNA, perhaps because stories allow us to vicariously live beyond our own limited mortal experience. Certainly stories are something human beings have been sharing since the days when cavemen and cavewomen first gathered around the firelight at night. They are a time-honored tradition and practically a birthright. And whether we're consciously aware of it or not, I believe their primal pull is this:

STORIES TEACH US HOW TO LIVE MORE FULLY

Stories are not just diversions; they are intimately woven into our lives in an endless multitude of ways. They not only entertain us, they inspire us, teach us, and can make us feel a part of something larger. They're the way religious and family traditions, history and principles are communicated and passed down from one generation to the next. They humanize us. The abstract is just that—abstract. Stories are the details, the specifics, and we human beings relate to one another via the details.

The wonderful website "Humans of New York" created by Brandon Stanton (if you're not familiar with it, **http://www. humansofnewyork.com**) is a great illustration of this principle. It takes a photo of a person on the street and in a seemingly simple, short paragraph or two tells you a lot about who they are via a few specific, often poignant details. The words and stories allow us to emotionally connect with them, their struggles and dreams, and often nudge us to contemplate something about our own lives as well. In the process, we're enriched.

And on a personal, vocational level, to be a writer seems a sort of glamorous occupation, at least on the surface of things, right? It conjures romantic notions of whipping up a masterpiece in some rustic cabin in the woods. There are no special tools required, a computer or even just old-school pen and paper will do. Plus there's always that outside chance that one can become rich and famous.

But anyone who's ever given writing a serious go soon comes to the undeniable realization that it's deceptively hard work, the sort of work that can easily drive one to Margaritaville long before it's five o'clock anywhere. And then they may start to wonder: Why do it at all?

Here are five good reasons I can come up with; you will undoubtedly discover your own.

1. You get to live more.
Anaïs Nin wrote, "We write to taste life twice, in the moment and in retrospect." And if your own life is not enough, or even if it is, as a writer of fiction you get to vicariously live the lives of your characters, play with your fantasies and maybe even see them brought to life.

I wrote the script for my film *Only You* in a small, characterless apartment on the westside of Los Angeles. I'd been to Italy once before and dreamed of returning. The characters in the movie went to Positano because *I* wanted to go to Positano. I got to live their fantasy adventure in my mind as I wrote it, and then got to live it—not to mention hang with Robert Downey Jr.—in reality. As the saying goes, it doesn't get much better. Writing is a way to experience, a way to live, more.

2. It's a way to stay sane.

We write to remind ourselves of things we thought we knew but have somehow forgotten in the rush of daily life. The simple act of putting one's thoughts and ideas down on paper helps you catch them, contemplate them, savor them.

And let's face it, we're all a little bit nuts, right? I mean, given the times we're living in, don't you think anyone who *isn't* a little bit nuts is a little bit nuts? So I say make your angst and pain and confusion work for you. Why should those things get a free ride? When it all gets to be too much, don your invisible writer's hat and start taking notes.

One of the great beauties of being a writer is that suddenly everything in life, even the crappiest, most miserable situation or experience, becomes potential material. If you choose to look at life from a certain angle, it's all grist for the mill. I think in some way this ability to take a step back and mine our own experience, to find the humor and share the pain, is our consolation for being the more sensitive, contemplative types that writers, by nature, often tend to be.

Isak Dinesen, in her book, *Out of Africa*, wrote, "All suffering is bearable if it is seen as part of a story." There is a principle in meditation of mentally identifying with the witness to one's thoughts, not with the thoughts themselves. To me, putting on your invisible writer's hat is a somewhat similar exercise. If you can manage to do this, to take this mental step back and see your life through the lens of your creative writer's eye, it often has the side benefit of making many daily irritating situations seem somehow comical or at least more tolerable and even the larger losses and pain slightly more bearable.

So, exercise your writer's consciousness. Take your neuroses, your fears and dreams, your secret wish, the most humiliating thing that you wouldn't want anyone to know, and put them down on the page. You can always cut them later. But remember that often these confidences and revelations make for the best stories. They can be what other people relate to the most, heartened to discover that somebody else has been there too. Filmmaker Joss Whedon says, "Whatever makes you weird is probably your greatest asset." And if you can manage to make people laugh at themselves, take themselves a little more lightly, I believe there are what a friend used to call "bonus points in heaven" for you.

3. You have a great excuse to explore and learn and observe.
For my former boss, director Sydney Pollack, making a movie was a way to explore a thematic life question that intrigued him. What question do you want to know the answer to? As a writer, you now officially have license to explore anything and everything you've ever wondered about and justify it as research.

When it comes to finding inspiration, take note of what you love and what you hate. Dorothea Brande, in her terrific book, *On Becoming a Writer*, advises that whatever inspires strong emotion in you, either positive or negative, deserves your attention. She adds, "Try to be one of those people on whom nothing is lost." To me, that's another way of saying be present, be mindful.

And on the subject of mindfulness, a slight digression here. I'm a big Ernest Hemingway fan. Okay, sure, there's the philandering and the alcoholism, the excessive machismo and wild animal slaughter (special condolences to the bulls of Spain, the elephants of Africa and the marlins in the Gulf Stream. Though, on balance, he did seem to quite adore his kitty cats.) Regardless, then there is the *writing*, and that's the only reason we care about any of the rest of it.

So I was excited when, years ago, I happened across a collection of articles he wrote while working as a reporter, some before he achieved great fame as a novelist and some after, titled *Byline: Ernest Hemingway.*

The excerpt below is from an essay he wrote for *Esquire* magazine in 1935, when he was thirty-six. It details the advice he gave to a young man who'd hitchhiked from Minnesota down to Key West and shown up on his doorstep, claiming he wanted to be a writer. Hemingway gave the kid a job as night watchman on his boat, the Pilar, and was from then on pestered endlessly about what he calls, "the practice of letters." Because the kid played the violin, (badly), Hemingway nicknamed him Maestro, which he then shortened to "Mice."

Here is an excerpt from "Monologue to the Maestro." Hemingway refers to himself as "Y.C.," short for "Your Correspondent."

Mice: *How can a writer train himself?*

Y.C.: *Watch what happens today. If we get into a fish see exactly what it is that everyone does. If you get a kick out of it while he is jumping remember back until you see exactly what the action was that gave you the emotion. Whether it was the rising of the line from the water and the way it tightened like a fiddle string until drops started from it, or the way he smashed and threw water when he jumped. Remember what the noises were and what was said. Find what gave you the emotion: what the action was that gave you the excitement. Then write it down making it clear so the reader will see it too and have the same feeling that you had. That's a five finger exercise.*

Mice: *All right.*

Y.C.: *Then get into somebody else's head for a change.*

If I bawl you out try to figure what I'm thinking about as well as how you feel about it. If Carlos curses Juan think what both their sides of it are. Don't just think who is right. As a man things are as they should or shouldn't be. As a man you know who is right and who is wrong. You have to make decisions and enforce them. As a writer you should not judge. You should understand.

Mice: All right.

Y.C.: Listen now. When people talk listen completely. Don't be thinking what you're going to say. Most people never listen. Nor do they observe. You should be able to go into a room and when you come out know everything you saw there and not only that. If that room gave you any feeling you should know exactly what it was that gave you that feeling. Try that for practice. When you're in town stand outside the theater and see how the people differ in the way they get out of taxis or motor cars. There are a thousand ways to practice. And always think of other people.

What I particularly love about this piece is not only its slightly jaundiced yet still good-natured wit, but also that the writing advice is real and good and honest. It might not be about screenwriting, per se, but the knowledge imparted, particularly about paying attention, is valuable for any writer, artist, or for that matter for any human being.

4. You get to share your life experience. You get to "be what you've come here for."

I think writers as a species tend to be outsiders. We're more often observers than participants, sometimes recluses even. But deep down, I think what everyone craves is to live more. As the novelist E.M. Forster famously observed, the goal is to "only connect." And when you do that, when you're able to capture and effectively communicate what is true for you, you feel less alone, and you make your audience feel the same way. Those are the moments of sheer creative exhilaration, when you feel the wind at your back and it's almost as if you're channeling something that's coming not so much from you as through you.

I believe it's a writer's job to tell the truth as we see it. Somebody's got to do it, right? But admittedly this sort of behavior can sometimes tend make one a teensy bit unpopular around, say, performance review time or the Thanksgiving dinner table. (Unless, of course, you have the gift of being extraordinarily funny about it. The court jester always gets away with murder.) Regardless, on the page you are free. You might want to change the names, but here's your chance. Go ahead and put whatever you want to say in your characters' mouths; you're not saying these things, *they* are. And on a related note, if you're one of those mere mortals who comes up with the perfect comeback twenty-four hours too late, then, ah, my friend, writing is for you.

5. If you work really hard and you're really lucky, you get to add meaning and pleasure to the lives of others.

If your goal is to write a movie, let's assume you've got two hours of somebody's—ideally, millions of somebodies'—precious time. What do you want them to know? To feel? To understand? Doing creative work is about adding meaning to your life, and in the process, ideally adding meaning to the lives of others.

A now a brief word about critics:

They have their place. *I guess*... And some of them—dear, lovely, departed Roger Ebert, I'm talking about you—bring a vast understanding of the art form as well as their own unique sensibility, passion, sensitivity and intelligence to the table. Still, the Eberts of the world are the exception. Never forget that writing about writing is a hell of a lot easier than *writing*. Trust me, I've done both. And talking about it is easier still. Everybody's got an opinion, especially online, everybody's a critic. You must shut them out, certainly while you're in the early stages, and this includes your mean inner one, too. And always remember, "Nobody ever erected a statue to a critic."

Finally, sometimes the many masters—commercial, structural, financial, personal, logistical, emotional, intellectual, spiritual and otherwise—one has to try to serve in the process of writing, especially writing for Hollywood, can feel overwhelming. It can be tough and disheartening, and you may find yourself asking, why bother? When that happens, remember that the real goal is for you to exercise your creativity and share your own unique vision, experience and imagination. The real meaning is found in playing with your dreams and neuroses, your fears and joys and giving them life on the page; it's found in living a creative life.

Write to remind the rest of us that we are not alone. Write what you know to be true.

Recommended WATCH: Writer Elizabeth Gilbert's (Big Magic, Creative Living Beyond Fear; The Signature of All Things; Eat, Pray, Love) TED talk about your creative genius. (**http://www.ted.com/talks/elizabeth_gilbert_on_genius**)

CHAPTER TWO

WHAT MOVIES ARE REALLY ABOUT
And the Moral to (Almost) Every Story

> *"Movies are about the moment when somebody's life changed."*
>
> ~ Christopher Walken

T HAT ONE SENTENCE IS ABOUT as good and succinct a description of what makes a movie as I've ever come across. Whether you're talking about a big-budget studio blockbuster or a quirky indie with a more complex or unconventional narrative, it's an incredibly helpful idea to keep in mind.

Obviously, there are exceptions to every rule. One can choose to write a movie about virtually anything. It is, as they say, a free country. Terrence Malick can make movies that are more visual meditations and mood pieces than conventional plot-driven narratives. You can shoot six hours of somebody sleeping, as Andy Warhol did, and call it a movie. And it's great that these sorts of exceptions exist, but exceptions are exceptional for a reason. If you're not independently wealthy enough to finance your own project and your goal is to sell a screenplay to someone who will pay to produce it, or to convince someone to give you the money to shoot your own film, you should have some understanding of what larger audiences and most people who finance movies consider commercially viable.

If you've been to a multiplex recently, you might say movies are about superheroes, zombies, 3D, explosions—oh, and more superheroes. Or maybe they're about men who will be boys. Or, if you're more a fan of art house/indie fare, you might say they're about period romances and historical figures and injustices. And all of these would be correct. Movies are, of course, about all of those things, and fortunately plenty more. But if you boil it all down, if you change the names and dates and places and specifics, what almost all movies are fundamentally about is this: **the moment when somebody's life changed.**

Notice that they're not typically about someone's *entire* life. All sorts of things have obviously usually come before, and one assumes will come after we, the audience, are given this limited window into a particular character's life. But the slice of time in which we are most interested, the one that is the most dramatically charged, is the moment when somebody's life changed. And usually as a result of this life change, this shift in the outer circumstances, the somebody changes as well.

Accepting this premise leads to at least a couple of significant questions:

Question 1: Why, exactly, do characters change?
And the answer, almost always, is: *Because they have a problem.*

Question 2: How, exactly, do they change?
Ah, that is for you, the creator, to decide.

We know that most people resist change, generally because it's damn hard work. So, most of us, fictional characters included, usually have to be in some way forced into it. Why would we change unless things have somehow become untenable? If it ain't broke, right? Consequently, something must be broken for your hero in order for you to have a story. Drama is conflict, and something must be or go awry in your hero's life in order to propel him into action.

> *Movies are about that moment when a character is forced to rise to the occasion—to sink or to swim.*

Regarding your hero: It's been said that if he doesn't have a problem, *you*, the writer, have a problem. I'd take that adage a step further and add that if he doesn't have a *specific* problem, you have a problem. So it is your job as the writer to really put the screws to your hero; to confront him with a dilemma, thereby putting pressure on him and forcing him into a situation in which he really has no choice but to take some sort of action, and thus usually ultimately to change and evolve in the process.

Here's another description of what makes a movie that I like:

Somebody wants something really badly and goes after it against all odds.

If this definition is helpful for you, you'll want to think about establishing who that somebody is to start with. How does he see the world? How does he relate to other people? Is he honest or dishonest? Rich or poor? Lonely or popular? Cynical or romantic? Is he in some way an underdog?

And however good or bad he may be in subjective moral terms, what is it he needs to learn in order to live more fully? In what way might he need to change to somehow live a freer life? How does he need to grow? How might he be somehow different by the end of the story?

Then, given who he is when the story begins, what's the worst thing that could happen to him? An underlying lesson of story is that often what seems to be the worst possible thing that could befall someone ultimately turns out to be the best thing that could've happened to him. It was the push he needed from the universe to grow and move in a new direction and to a new level in his life.

Also, you'll want to identify what exactly is the "something" your hero wants. Ideally, you'll want to pin down a specific goal. Of course we'd all like to be happy and healthy and rich and famous, etc. but that's not what movies are generally about.

Instead, they're about the *specific manifestation* of these larger goals that people seek: the love of a particular person; a job or victory of some specific sort, the list is infinite. This specificity is necessary because the story really *is* in the details, and also because it allows the audience to understand whether the hero has achieved his goal by the end of the movie.

Regardless, by the time the final credits roll, ideally something is different. The hero *himself* is different. He has gained something internally, some knowledge about himself and/or the world, and has grown in some way, perhaps even a small way, that frees him to live more fully. Or not. And if not, what you have on your hands is usually called a tragedy.

Think about that word for a second: "tragedy." Isn't it a rather interesting commentary on life that when people don't change and don't grow, it's by definition a tragedy? And some of our most powerful and profound films are tragic. But if you want to err on the side of caution, commercially speaking, you will probably want to leave your viewers with at least a shred of hope.

Legendary screenwriter William Goldman (*All the Presidents Men, Butch Cassidy and the Sundance Kid, The Princess Bride, Misery,* etc.) in his book *Adventures in the Screen Trade,* asserts, "People want to believe nice things." Almost everybody likes a happy ending, provided—and this is key—it's an *earned* happy ending. We're satisfied if we feel that the hero has fought and worked hard to achieve whatever it is he ultimately gets. In stories, as in life, we tend to be irritated by people who are simply handed everything, and we tend to admire and respect those who work hard for what they accomplish and gain. And this brings me to one more useful definition of a story:

A story is an emotion-producing machine.

People go to movies to *feel* something. Life can often be mundane, routine and numbing, if not downright painful. As Sydney Pollack's exasperated agent tells Dustin Hoffman's too earnest unemployed actor in *Tootsie*, "Nobody wants to pay twenty bucks to watch people living next to chemical waste. They can see that in New Jersey!" You need to be delivering more than what people can see everyday. You need to give them a reason to genuinely feel something: laughter, heart-pounding suspense, profound emotion, excitement, etc. and thereby—and this is the important part—*to feel more alive.* That's the experience they're paying you for.

So, here's one final principle to keep in mind as you ponder story ideas:

Drama is conflict. We go to movies to watch somebody fight.

> "'The cat sat on a mat' is not a story. 'The cat sat on the dog's mat' is a story."
>
> ~ John LeCarre

Having spent a good many years both analyzing material and creating my own, I was surprised that it was only when I began teaching screenwriting that I fully recognized the significance of this basic axiom of drama. Whether we are consciously aware of it or not, from a certain angle, the reason we plunk down our cash and spend our precious leisure time in a movie theater (or streaming films at home) is to watch somebody struggle. We pay to see someone fight to overcome the obstacles in his life and, ideally, to transcend them and in the process be himself somehow transformed.

We go to watch someone fight, both internally and externally; to fight for survival, for love, for dignity, for acceptance, for freedom, for justice, for respect and self-respect. These are the larger, more universal goals we all understand and desire. The specifics change, but as the song goes, "the fundamental things apply." And the harder the hero has to fight, the more engaged we are likely to become.

You know how sometimes the universe just seems to pile on and kick your ass? That's what movies are about, the point in life at which the universe really kicks someone's ass. So, we go to watch characters fight back but, more important, we go to see them in some way *overcome* the obstacles life throws at them, and in that process somehow become "better," more self-realized human beings. We go to watch someone conquer not only the enemy without but also the enemy within. We go to watch them learn how to live more fully.

On a very fundamental level, seeing this drama played out over and over again in endless permutations is comforting and pleasurable. And by mentally stepping into a character's shoes for a couple of hours, we not only get a brief respite from our own troubles, we also can be made to feel we're not alone in them. And, by implication, we can see that our problems may not be so bad after all and that whatever they may be, we too might overcome them.

I believe that pretty much everyone on the planet sees herself or himself, to a greater or lesser extent, as an underdog. For even for the most fortunate among us there's inevitably some struggle, suffering, pain and after all that, waiting at the end, sooner or later—dammit—is death. As the saying goes, no one gets out of this alive. And no one is coming to save us. It is up to us to save ourselves, and so we take immense vicarious pleasure, we take heart, from watching a character do precisely that.

Thus, the obstacles you create and throw in the path of your hero are truly there to bring him to a higher realization of himself. They are there to teach him something. And this is the larger lesson of stories, whether it's overt or not: By learning how to confront, deal with and overcome the obstacles in our lives, we can grow as human beings and add meaning to our existence.

Which leads me to the inherent lesson, or "moral," underlying most all stories:

What matters most in life is not what happens to us, but what we do about it.

Stories are about transcendence. They're about someone finding out that he is stronger than he thought he was. Thus, the obstacles in our characters' lives are there to quite literally *build character*. So, you don't want to just give your characters a happy ending, you want to make them *earn* it. Don't make things easy on them. Make them work, make them struggle and fight hard to prove how badly they want something before you finally reward them in the end. Remember, "The harder the struggle, the more glorious the triumph."

There is, I think, a universal, almost primal longing to always feel as though we're somehow moving forward in life. The deep desire to believe that we can overcome our obstacles and that the struggles we face in our daily lives are not meaningless or in vain but can somehow help bring us to a higher realization of ourselves is incredibly powerful. If in your storytelling you can create specifics that tap into these universal struggles and desires in a convincing and authentic way, you will truly have something special.

STORY OVERVIEW TAKEAWAYS:

1. Movies are about the moment when somebody's life changed.

2. Stories are emotion-producing machines.

3. The obstacles in a hero's life are there to build character.

4. By the end of the story, as a result of having taken the journey of the story, usually the hero is changed as a human being; he's grown somehow, even if in a small way.

5. The underlying moral to most best-loved stories is this: What matters most in life isn't so much what happens to us, it's what we *do* about it.

STORY OVERVIEW WORKSHEET - QUESTIONS TO GET YOU THINKING:

1. Who is my hero and how does he see and relate to the world?

2. What specific problem can I give him that will in some way compel him to change?

3. Has he identified a particular goal and is he going to have to fight hard to achieve it?

4. Does he need to change as a human being in order to solve his problem and achieve his goal? What does he need to learn; how might he need to grow?

5. How might the journey of the story and the obstacles he faces over the course of it force him to do that?

CHAPTER THREE

WHAT'S THE BIG IDEA? Finding Your Concept

> *"Ask me if I care."*
>
> ~ Anonymous thirteen-year-old, and pretty
> much any executive in Hollywood

S O YOU'VE DECIDED YOU WANT to write a screenplay. Excellent. Now, what exactly do you want to write about? You may already have a clear sense, and that's great, but if you're not yet entirely sure, don't worry. There are a number of strategies you can employ to get the inspiration flowing. Here are five to consider.

FIVE IDEA-GENERATING STRATEGIES:

1. What philosophical or thematic question do *you* want to know the answer to?

Your work obviously does and must come out of you and your own life experience. It springs from your spirit, your heart and mind, the things *you* are interested in and care passionately about. Really, what else are you to draw from? So one way to approach this is to write out of a deep need to explore something that you care about, or a question to which you want to know the answer.

Michael Arndt, the Academy Award-winning screenwriter of *Little Miss Sunshine*, (among other movies, including *Toy Story 3*), has said that he was inspired to write LMS after reading an interview with Arnold Schwarzenegger wherein Schwarzenegger declared, "If there's one thing in this world I hate, it's losers. I despise them."

Arndt was so incensed by the idea of dismissing and labeling other people as losers that he wanted, as he put it, to "attack that idea at its core." His script and subsequent film did just that in brilliant satirical, yet touching, fashion.

2. "Seed scenes" inspiration

I recently came across this concept in a Scriptmag.com article by a writer named Clive Davies-Frayne. Before you find yourself waist deep in Act II conflicts, obstacles, and (alas) sometimes story problems, something has to light a fire in you to make you want to tell a particular story.

Inspiration can of course come from anywhere, at any time. But even if you don't have that big philosophical question in mind yet, one thing you'll want to pay particular attention to and hold onto are what Davies-Frayne calls "seed scenes." These are the scenes that almost *do* write themselves. These are the ones that easily come to you when you have a particular idea, the ones that create a spark in you and make you eager to sit down and write your story. He calls it "visualizing little flashes of story." These scenes can help you refine your concept and get your story moving forward.

For me, a critical seed scene in writing *What Women Want* was the moment when Mel Gibson's character first realizes what's happening to him—that he's hearing the private, inner thoughts of the women all around him—and it completely freaks him out. He frantically confides in his best friend, who is the first one to recognize and articulate the true beauty of the situation: that Mel now knows *what women want*. And then, with a touch of awe in his voice adds, "You could rule the world."

Coming up with that scene was not only fun and inspiring, it was a guiding light for me, as it not only encapsulated what the movie was about, it felt fun, funny, and tonally like what I was aiming for.

3. Think in terms of tone and genre of your favorite films

You may not know your exact story details yet, but usually you have a general sense of the kind of movie you want to write, of its overall tone. And if you don't, then this is one of the things you'll want to consider before you embark on writing your script.

What are the movies that you could watch over and over again? What movies make you want to write movies? If you haven't already, make a list and look for the commonalities. If you love comedy, chances are that's probably a genre you'll want to consider. If horror is more your thing, then maybe you'll want to think in terms of evils and phobias. This may seem rather obvious, but it's a way to begin brainstorming and narrowing things down.

A friend of mine, Kim Krizan, who co-wrote the beautiful films *Before Sunrise* and *Before Sunset* with director Richard Linklater and whose screenwriting class I once had the pleasure of sitting in on, asserts that the movies you personally relate to the most are thematically telling your own story in some way. If you stand back, she says, you'll see there's a consistency in what you're drawn to. And the deeper you go into the specifics and emotions of your own story, the more you'll hit that universal vein.

4. "What ifs?"

Another idea-generating strategy, especially for high-concept, fantasy and supernatural movies, is to think in terms of magical "what ifs?" and then play the outcome for real.

I've found that, for whatever reason, I like to play with the "what if?" of what I call "universal fantasies." *Only You* was one of those: what if your soul mate really existed and you were given his name? So was *What Women Want*. What if men could read women's minds? I mean, what man or woman hasn't wished that in one form or another at some point?

Further on that subject, *What Women Want* was inspired in part by the beautiful and touching German film *Wings of Desire* by Wim Wenders, in which an angel has the ability to hear people's innermost thoughts. That concept coupled with small moment I had on vacation years ago that, for whatever reason, stayed with me.

I'd gone to the Bahamas and happened to strike up a flirtation with a guy who was working at the resort where I was staying. Unfortunately, this was in January, and while I was in what was ostensibly the sun-drenched tropics, a freak arctic storm, the kind that freezes all the orange crops, swept through Florida and down into the Caribbean. Thus it was actually colder on my vacation in the Bahamas that week than it was back home in Los Angeles. Oh well. Anyway, as you might imagine, there's not a whole lot to do in a tropical resort when it's rainy, windy and in the high 40's, and most guests were, not surprisingly, cranky. So, the resort staff set up movies indoors.

This guy brought popcorn and champagne, which was lovely. But more than that, there was this tiny moment when I was sitting in one of those big rattan chairs—you know the ones with the big fan backs?—and though I'm fairly tall, my feet didn't quite touch the ground. I was just barely on the brink of noticing this, honestly the thought hadn't yet even quite fully formed in my mind that I was a little uncomfortable, when he slid a footstool over in front of me. It was a small gesture, but it struck me that he knew not only what I wanted, he knew it even before *I* knew it. It was as though he'd *read my mind*. (Or maybe he'd just had practice. Be that as it may.)

There were a couple of lines of dialogue in my original script which, alas, didn't make it into the final film, but which always amused me and were part of another seed scene. I had Mel Gibson's character, in sheer exasperation, say to his girlfriend who was mad at him, "Just tell me what you want—I'll say it. I'll do it. I'll buy it." And her response was, "If I tell you what to do and then you do it, it's not the same."

As ridiculous as that sounds, somehow it's true, right? You don't want to have to tell someone to buy you flowers, or hold the door, or do whatever little thoughtful thing, you just want them to *know*. Once I came up with the idea of a man who was actually able to really *know*, I heard Freud's classic phrase in my head: "*what women want*" and I knew I was onto something.

A few more "what if" examples:

- What if all the musty old objects in the museum came to life after dark? (*Night at the Museum*)

- What if you could create a living dinosaur? (*Jurassic Park*, and now, of course, *Jurassic World*.) I think this is one of the better movie concepts I've ever heard. First, it seems *almost* real, almost possible, and that plausibility makes it that much more intriguing. And it's something that appeals to every kid and the kid in all of us. It also lends itself to amazing visuals and special effects, adventure, etc. A truly brilliant idea for a film, even if it was a novel first.

- What if you could travel back in time and change history? (*Back to the Future, The Terminator movies* and many more)

- What if children's toys came alive when humans were not around and had their own lives and relationships? (*Toy Story*)

- What if vampires really existed and you fell in love with one? (*Twilight*)

- What if ghosts really existed and there were people whose 9-5 job was to get rid of them? (*Ghostbusters*)

- What if wizards really existed and there was a secret academy they attended as children to learn their trade? (*Harry Potter movies*)

- What if zombies really existed? (Too many to name)

5. Other sources of inspiration, or IRL

Maybe you're fascinated by a particular period in history, or a specific real-life character. Start with some research and see if you can emotionally connect to them. You might also see if you can identify the critical window of time when that person's life changed, and which is thus best suited to motion picture dramatization.

And wherever your inspiration comes from, here's something else to bear in mind: Dare to be personal. I once saw writer/director Judd Apatow speak at the Writers Guild, and he brought a clip from the TV show *Freaks and Geeks* which he'd co-created years before. He said that this scene was the first really personal one he ever wrote, and that more people responded to this little scene to than anything else he had done prior to it. Then he urged us to, "be generous with your life experience." It's very simple, but I think it's pretty brilliant and moving. I encourage you to take a look.

Recommended WATCH: Apatow's Freaks and Geeks scene.
(https://www.youtube.com/watch?v=cmCpmEQD0L4)

Remember that your job as a writer, in its simplest terms, is to make the audience care. Andrew Stanton, Pixar writer and director extraordinaire (*Toy Story* 1, 2, 3 & upcoming 4, *Finding Nemo, Wall-E* and many more) maintains in his TED talk that the greatest story commandment is "make me care."

Film critic Roger Ebert called movies, "a machine that generates empathy." In the documentary film *Life Itself*, he says, "Movies are the most powerful empathy machine in all the arts. We all are born with a certain package. We are who we are: where we were born, who we were born as, how we were raised. We're kind of stuck inside that person, and the purpose of civilization and growth is to be able to reach out and empathize a little bit with other people. And for me, the movies are like a machine that generates empathy. It lets you understand a little bit more about different hopes, aspirations, dreams and fears. It helps us to identify with the people who are sharing this journey with us."

So, if a story is an emotion-producing machine, think about what emotions you want to evoke in your audience. And on that subject, most experts on writing will advise you to write what you know. For one thing, it's simply easier, and I think it's more rewarding and ultimately has more emotional resonance for the viewer. *But* this doesn't have to be literal. The guys who wrote *Toy Story* weren't toys. Nor, to my knowledge, were any of them cowboys or astronauts. But they knew and understood what it was to feel abandoned, jealous, heartbroken. And they also knew how it felt to be part of a team, to have a mission. They brought all of that authentic *emotional knowledge* and then some to bear on the characters and the story.

Ricky Gervais, the brilliant co-creator of *The Office* and *Extras*, among other series, has a terrific short video on this subject and about his writing process. He describes an experience he had at the age of thirteen with an English teacher who kept telling him to, "write what you know," and how, with the inadvertent help of an elderly neighbor, he reluctantly became a believer in that philosophy. I strongly encourage you to check it out.

Recommended WATCH: Ricky Gervais on his writing process.
(https://www.youtube.com/watch?v=zTJyDe7a2bo)

Finally, try not to overthink it. Really what a story is about, for our movie-creation purposes anyway, is a character to whom something happens, and who then then has to try to rise to the occasion and deal with this change or event as best he can. That's it, in a very pared-down nutshell.

You may have a particular character you want to explore, or a world or time period that intrigues you, or a philosophical question you're curious about. Great, go with that, and ask yourself questions about it. What might a person like this want? How might a person in this situation need to grow? What's the worst thing that could happen to him? With whom might he conflict? What might he need to learn?

If instead of a character it's a situation that you want to explore, who might be the most ill-prepared for this turn of events? Who might have the furthest to go in terms of how he needs to change? How would he seek to deal with whatever is thrown at him? What obstacles might he run into?

Keep asking questions until you hit on something you spark to, and then ask some more. It's like working with clay or creating a painting: You work it and build it, little by little. You try something, go back, erase it, and try something else.

For the record, the script for *Tootsie* took three years and at least five different writers, and Sydney Pollack, to develop, and this is people at the top of their game. *Toy Story* has seven credited writers. The writer of *The King's Speech*, David Seidler, who had researched his story for years, claims that once the director came on board he wrote fifty more drafts. *Fifty.*

My point is that screenwriting can be a deceptively challenging craft, but it's all a process. There's a saying in yoga, "You are where you need to be." Start there and just keep building, keep moving forward.

FINDING YOUR CONCEPT TAKEAWAYS:

1. Inspiration can be found in a multitude of ways and places. These include:

   - Questions about life to which you want to know the answer
   - Seed scenes
   - Your favorite films
   - What ifs?
   - Art, history/true stories
   - Real life and/or a combination of all of the above

2. Writing that is personal is the most powerful kind, but remember that "personal" doesn't have to mean literal.

---

3. Your main job as a writer is to make the audience care.

4. Writing is a process.

FINDING YOUR CONCEPT WORKSHEET:

1. Make a list of at least fifty of your favorite films. Pay attention to any commonalities.

2. Take your thinking about your list a step further and see if you can pin down *why* these movies are your favorites. What, specifically, do you love about them?

3. What life question do you want to know the answer to? What inspires strong emotion in you, good or bad? Again, make yourself a list.

4. What's your greatest fantasy? What's your greatest fear?

CHAPTER FOUR

CREATING A LOG LINE

"It's better to do a bad job on a good idea than the inverse."

~ Billy Wilder

O NCE YOU'VE IDENTIFIED A CONCEPT you'd like to work on, you'll want to try to encapsulate the idea into a sentence or two, into what's called a "log line" or "one-liner." Log lines serve a couple of important purposes: first, they enable you to pitch your project to agents, managers, producers, etc., as quickly and concisely as possible.

Equally if not more important, when they're done right, they're a tool you can use to help keep you and your story on track. They're a shorthand guide to hold your scenes up against as you progress to be sure you're not getting lost along the way.

Log lines are generally no more than two to three sentences long and are intended to communicate the essence of your story idea, but they can be surprisingly difficult to write. This is the case for a number of reasons, including:

1. You have to try to somehow convey what will ultimately cover roughly 110 pages in just a few sentences.

2. Ideally, a log line should be intriguing and should sound like it has the potential to actually become a movie.

3. You have to have a strong handle on the movie you intend to write in order to be able to encapsulate it into a compelling sentence or two. It might seem counterintuitive,

but it's amazing how any overall weaknesses in your larger story can make themselves painfully apparent when you try to boil everything down to just a couple of sentences.

In fact, if you can't boil your idea down to a couple of sentences, even if you're not aiming for "high concept," I can make a strong case that you're not yet fully ready to write your script. Now maybe you're the next Jim Brooks or Richard Linklater or Nicole Holofcener, and your stuff is really more character- and dialogue-driven. You'd better be though, because, alas, there simply isn't much room in the business at this point for work of this nature. You'd better also be a talented director and/or good at raising your own money, and that's a high bar.

Even the extremely gifted Cameron Crowe (writer/director of *Jerry Maguire*, *Almost Famous*, and *Say Anything*, among other great films) who has an undeniable flair for creating memorable characters and smart, witty dialogue has been known to falter when it comes to the crux of what some of his more recent movies are really about.

His latest film, *Aloha*, suffers from a lack of clear narrative focus and solid structure. I can't help but wonder what the log line for this movie looked like, given the very mixed bag of ideas and plot lines it seemed to be trying to contain and address that never quite coalesced into a cohesive tale. This just goes to show that even for the most talented among us, it can be far too easy to wander off track.

As you brainstorm and explore ideas and begin to narrow things down, you'll want to be sure to hold yourself to a high enough standard before you set out on your 110-page journey. Billy Wilder's advice at the beginning of this chapter has never been more true. For better or worse, in today's market there is a greater emphasis than ever on concept. Brainstorm with abandon and then choose carefully the ideas you want to develop and focus on, run them by people you trust, and be selective. I'm not saying to be crassly commercial. What I'm saying is that before you set out on a long journey, you want to be sure you've chosen a worthwhile destination.

Ideally, you want to have a firm sense of who and what your story is really about at its core and, better still, have what is called a **hook**, something that makes your story feel unique and compelling. What makes the description of it memorable and fresh? What about this particular idea have we not seen before? What will intrigue us and cause us to want to know more? And whatever that element is, whatever hook you manage to come up with, it most likely ought to show up in your log line.

I think one of the best ways to begin learning how to write log lines is by first trying writing them for movies you already know and love. Imagine you're charged with writing the TV Guide description for a few of your favorite movies.

LOG LINE EXAMPLES:

- *Tootsie:* "A desperately unemployed, self-involved actor puts on a dress in order to get a job. In the process of impersonating a woman, he gradually becomes a better man."

- *Toy Story:* "A cowboy doll gets jealous when a new spaceman toy shows up and threatens his position as the number one toy in a little boy's room."

- *The 40-Year-Old Virgin:* Talk about your high-concept ideas, this one says it all right there in just the five word title. If you want a slightly more elaborate version, "A painfully shy 40-year-old virgin is determined to finally get laid."

- *Argo:* "During the 1979 Iranian revolution, a resourceful CIA officer comes up with a bold plan to help six American diplomats escape the country disguised as a Canadian film crew there to scout a science fiction movie." (Based on a true story).

- *Iron Man:* "A cocky billionaire, weapons designer and war profiteer is taken captive in Afghanistan. After managing to escape by building an "Iron Man" super suit, he realizes he wants to do more than sell weapons to destroy the world; instead he wants to try to save it."

- *Thelma & Louise:* "Two law-abiding, mild-mannered women wind up running for their lives on a cross-country crime spree after one of them shoots and kills a would-be rapist."

- *The King's Speech:* "The Duke of York, who suffers from a severe speech impediment, is terrified to find himself unexpectedly thrust into the spotlight and the position of king of England when his father, King George V, dies, and his brother abdicates to marry an American divorcee." (Also based on a true story.)

- *Roman Holiday:* "A young princess on a world tour, feeling imprisoned by her overly regimented life, sneaks out of the palace incognito and goes AWOL in Rome. There she meets an American reporter who realizes he's stumbled onto the story of a lifetime and falls in love."

- *Shakespeare in Love:* Marc Norman, the original writer of this script, says he got this idea from his son, who called him from college and pitched it to him in just four words: "Will Shakespeare, Struggling Writer." That's an even shorter than usual log line, but I think it manages to intrigue the listener. It gives you the (world famous) protagonist and his struggle, and at the same time conveys a sense of fun and irony.

- *What Women Want:* "A chauvinistic advertising executive has a freak accident that enables him to read women's minds. Suddenly, for the first time in his life, he truly knows *what women want.*"

- *Mr. & Mrs. Smith:* Two professional secret agent assassins, unhappily married to each other and unaware that they're in the same profession, belatedly learn that their spouse is their biggest competition."

- *Erin Brockovich:* "An unemployed single mother gets a low-level filing job at a law firm and ultimately almost single-handedly brings down a California power company accused of polluting a city's water supply." (Yet another based on a true story.)

- *It's a Wonderful Life:* "A good, honest man finds himself accused of a crime he didn't commit and, in desperate circumstances, wishes he'd never been born. About to commit suicide, he is rescued by his guardian angel who shows him all he's contributed to the lives of others, and thus rediscovers his will to live."

Log lines can be tricky. Because they are so brief, every word is critical and there's a lot of you want to try to convey in those few words. You need to communicate at least the following:

1. Who your hero or protagonist is.

2. Some sense of his dilemma/struggle/goal; what this movie is going to be about.

3. A sense of the tone of your story. If you're writing a comedy, ideally your log line will be somehow amusing or at the least hint at the potential for laughs. The same goes if it's an idea for thriller or a horror movie: Can the listener easily imagine its potential to be suspenseful/scary?

4. Ideally something that is intriguing, something that feels fresh, a "hook"; something that makes us want to know more.

Once you've come up with a working log line, you'll want to move onto the next step of building out and structuring your story into three acts. We'll delve further into that in the next chapter.

LOG LINE TAKEAWAYS:

1. A solid log line is critical and something you want to be able to effectively articulate before you start writing your script.

2. A good log line communicates who the story is primarily about, a sense of what his struggle is, the genre/tone of the story, and ideally a hook that feels fresh.

3. A strong log line is both an important marketing tool and useful guide for helping to keep your story on track.

LOG LINE WORKSHEET:

1. Can you create a log line of one or two sentences that communicates the essence of your story?

2. Is your hero included in it?

3. Does it contain an adjective or two that describes your hero? Something that gives us a mental picture of who he is as a human being? ("mild-mannered, law-abiding women" in *Thelma & Louise*; "chauvinistic advertising executive" in *What Women Want*, etc.)

4. Is your log line both descriptive and intriguing?

5. Is it tonally in keeping with the story you're planning to tell? For example, if your script is to be a comedy, is it amusing? If it's a thriller or horror movie, does it sound scary or suspenseful?

6. Does it feel fresh? Does it feel like something we've not seen before in quite this way?

CHAPTER FIVE

STRUCTURING YOUR STORY INTO THREE ACTS;
(Spoiler: "It Helps If You Have A Plot")

> *"Writing is like heading out over the open sea in a small boat. It helps if you have a plan and a course laid out."*
>
> ~ John Gardner

A FEW YEARS BACK, I WENT to see the writers of *The Hangover*, Jon Lucas and Scott Moore, speak on a panel of Writers Guild of America nominees. Yes, that is correct, *The Hangover* got a nomination for best original screenplay from the WGA.

A wildly successful bromance, *The Hangover* grossed over $450 million worldwide and thus far has spawned two sequels. Now, for a movie to make that kind of money, especially one that was not based on a best seller, a comic book, or any other previously marketed "intellectual property," but a completely original piece, it clearly has to have struck a significant chord with audiences. And for it to get a nomination, it has to have done the same with other writers as well.

So, what exactly makes this movie stand out and do that? First, it had an intriguing and novel structure. Like *Memento*, the story is told almost in reverse, as the previous night is pieced together like a mystery, all the while with the clear and urgent present goal of finding the groom before his wedding the following day. The writers described it as something of a monster movie in which viewers never actually see the monster (well, not until the final credits anyway) but hear about it throughout. They spoke of wanting to avoid the obvious cliches of bachelor parties and write, "a bachelor party movie without the bachelor party." Thus, they came up with what they termed the "Jason Bourne" angle. That novel way into the story, I believe, is a large part of what not only made the movie a big hit, but also led to the WGA nomination.

But here's the other critical thing they mentioned they'd rather belatedly learned in the process of writing it, and this is the main reason I bring this story up at all: *"It helps if you have a plot."*

In other words, after years of working in the film business, they discovered it's really handy to have a true driving narrative, a rock-solid plot, upon which to hang all your inspired bits and pieces of brilliance, witty dialogue, clever action, etc.

Those writers who tell you such a thing isn't necessary, that they just sit down every day and wait to see what happens, wait to see where their characters lead them are, uh, what's the word for that again? Oh, yeah, *liars*. Okay, or maybe novelists. And good for them if that's the case. The novel form allows some creative freedom to meander around, but meandering is not the name of the game in screenwriting. There's not a lot of room for wandering in 110 pages, especially in big-budget studio movies, and it's far too easy to wander off track. If you're talking independent film, the criteria are admittedly somewhat different and more flexible. Still, I'd argue that a solid narrative structure with forward momentum will almost always serve you well, whatever the scale or subject of the story you're telling.

Movies have a specific structure, one that is different from that of a novel or a play or a television show, despite how many of those tend to get turned into movies. A friend used to call screenplays a 110-page haiku. Give or take, that's pretty accurate.

Today's feature scripts generally run 110 pages or less, especially for those just starting out. Filmmakers like James Cameron or Quentin Tarantino can, of course, get away with much more, but

I wouldn't recommend it. Novels, on the other hand, can be 100 pages, or 1000, or more. And a television series is its own form; they can run one season or ten and allow the audience to revisit the characters once a week, or binge watch in a weekend. But movies, particularly the ones which make their way into the multiplexes or even the art house theaters, typically have a much more restricted form.

In addition, to not have some clear sense of where you're headed— that is, where your hero is headed, what he wants to achieve, some of the obstacles he'll encounter along the way, and where he'll ultimately wind up— is like heading out onto the open ocean in a rowboat. You're almost inevitably bound to get lost, run out of supplies and will be lucky if you ever make it back to shore alive, let alone to your desired destination.

Aristotle, in his "Poetics," was famously the first to lay out the **three-act structure** that has become the norm in moviemaking, and each part of which has a specific purpose:

- **Act I is the beginning or set-up**

- **Act II is the middle or body of the story**

- **Act III is the ending or resolution**

These three acts generally have the following characteristics:

- Act 1, the Set-Up, runs about 25 pages. It's where you introduce your hero, his status quo, establish his main problem and have him begin to take action to try to solve it.

- Act II, the Body of the Story, is about twice the length of Act I, or 50 pages. This is where the hero encounters unexpected obstacles and complications en route to his goal, and where most of the character evolution takes place.

- Act III, the Resolution, is about the same length as Act I, about 25 pages. It's where, ideally, the story doesn't simply end, but is "resolved." It's also where any questions posed by the first act are answered.

I'll elaborate further on this structure later in this chapter. In the meantime, here are a couple other things that are generally expected of motion picture screenplays:

1. Movies typically feature an active protagonist, or hero, who sets out to achieve something specific, his goal, over the course of the story.

2. Movies tend to fall into a particular **genre** (or maybe a few mixed or sub-genres): comedy, drama, action/adventure, horror, sci-fi, thriller, family, satire, western, etc.

A lot of this seems pretty obvious, right? Your hero has to have something to do, something he wants to try to achieve or we'd be watching two hours of a whole lot of nothing. Yet you'd be amazed at how many scripts lack these seemingly essential elements, or seem to repeat variations on the same scene over and over again.

Yes, these scripts all start somewhere; and yes, there's stuff in the middle, maybe lots of talking or lots of explosions and chases; and yes, they finally, in some cases mercifully, come to an end. But that's not the same thing as creating a story that's well laid out and told in purposeful order with a building narrative, a convincing character arc, and a satisfying resolution.

So, say you've identified your hero, given him a specific problem and goal of some sort, identified a character trait or two which it would behoove him to improve upon, maybe even thought of a number of supporting characters and generally what you want your story to be about, as well as its tone or genre.

Now what? Now something *happens*. Your hero is somehow put in motion. But it's important that what happens is not simply random. It's important that you structure your story in such a way that what happens to your hero forces him into action, action that requires him to ultimately learn and/or grow somehow in a way that he needs, and that from there the story builds organically to a resolution.

Screenwriter William Goldman has famously written, "Screenplays are structure." What is key is a solid foundation, a strong spine for your story, with a logical progression of essential scenes and events which will ultimately take your hero from Point A to his (usually new & improved) Point B.

Dialogue, on the other hand, although more immediately "visible" to the viewer, can fairly easily be changed. To me, dialogue is the equivalent of decor in the house, or the icing on the cake. It may be the first thing most people notice, but if the foundation of the house is crooked, or the cake is sliding off the plate, the color of paint on the walls or the pretty frosting flowers on top become somewhat immaterial.

Anyway, this means your hero should have a goal—not just a vague aspiration, but a clearly defined and specific goal. He shouldn't just want to be "rich and famous," he should want to win a particular contest, get a particular job, create a particular invention or work of art, win a particular fight, achieve a particular dream, win the heart of a particular person, etc. And generally the main engine of the plot, the thing that keeps your story moving forward, is your hero's pursuit of what he really, really wants—his pursuit of his goal.

Now let's take a look at each of these structural pieces in greater detail:

GENERAL LENGTH AND PURPOSE OF EACH ACT :
Act I: The Beginning or Set-Up of the Story, pages 1-25

Act I is where you introduce and set up your hero, how he typically behaves, and his world, where and how he lives. Is it past, present, future? Is it fantasy, gritty urban, the Wild West, suburban, outer space, a war zone, a tropical island, etc.? This is what we call his **status quo**.

Act I is also where you establish his dilemma, that is, the main problem he faces. His problems can and should escalate over the course of the story, but something should go wrong, somehow pressure should be put on him early in the first act, which then leads him to take some sort of action to try to (re)solve it.

You also want to identify his external goal, that is, the specific thing he thinks he **wants**. In *Tootsie*, Michael Dorsey thinks his problem is that he's unemployed. What he wants is a job. He doesn't think he **needs** to become a better man, or a more empathetic person. He doesn't go in search of these internal improvements. The ways in which he winds up changing as a human being are a *byproduct* of his pursuit of his external goal.

Finally, you'll want to establish his flaw, or the thing he needs (to learn) in character terms. That is, in what way does he need to change in order to live a "better," fuller, freer life?

Typically, the thing a character needs (to learn) tends to be larger, more emotionally related, and have something to do with how he looks at and lives his life. It quite literally has to do with his *character*. Whereas the thing he wants—his external goal—tends to be much more specific, finite and tangible.

The thing he wants is almost always specifically identified for the audience. The thing he needs should be clear as well, but generally isn't literally identified; it has more of a read-between-the-lines/add-up-the-pieces quality that we sense in terms of how someone might need to change with regard to how he relates to others and the world.

This thing the hero needs (to learn) is what informs what we call the **character arc**, the way in which he is transformed over the course of the story. Again, movies are about the moment where somebody's life changed—and not just the externals, but how the character himself is also changed.

In addition, there are two very important structural elements which typically occur in Act I and which you'll want to identify in your story:

1. THE INCITING INCIDENT, which usually occurs at about page 10.

Usually the first few opening scenes of a movie establish the way things have always been—the status quo. For better or worse, there is a sense of a world in equilibrium, or at least in stasis. Maybe it's a crappy world, maybe it's a great world, maybe it's just okay, but it's probably been this way for a while.

And then, about ten pages in, something happens; something changes. This something is called the Inciting Incident. This event in some way puts pressure on the hero and *incites* him to action.

Michael Arndt calls the Inciting Incident the "bolt from the blue." It's also known as the "cause for all that follows." Another good description might be, "a change in the status quo." Something shifts in the hero's world, and that shift somehow sets him in motion. Finally, a way I like to look at the Inciting Incident is: "If only this hadn't happened" (whatever "this" is), life would never have taken this turn. That is, the story would never have happened at all.

Quite often the Inciting Incident is something that the hero wishes hadn't happened which then forces him to take some sort of action to try to contend with it and then ultimately leads to his personal growth.

And that brings us to the second critical structural element in Act I:

2. PLOT POINT #1, which usually happens at about page 25.

So, first you establish the problem, the dilemma the hero is facing, usually as a result of the Inciting Incident. The pressure then builds on him throughout the rest of first act, so much so that by the end of Act I, he takes some sort of action to try to resolve his problem and achieve his goal.

The first act typically ends with this action, which is called Plot Point #1. Here's my own definition for that:

The action the hero takes to solve what he perceives his problem to be, which then results in unexpected consequences.

Okay, it's admittedly a little wordy, but all of these words are important. It is **action** the **hero** takes—something he does, not something he says—to **solve a problem** that then leads to **unexpected consequences**.

Do you know that Serenity Prayer? "God grant me the serenity to accept the things I cannot change, the courage to change the things I can, and the wisdom to know the difference."? Movies are about that second one, "the courage to change the things I can." Plot Point #1 is the taking of action; it is the attempt by the hero to, as Shakespeare put it, "Take arms against a sea of troubles and by opposing, end them."

So, at the end of Act I your hero takes some sort of ideally drastic action to try to solve whatever he perceives his problem to be. This action then typically spins the story in something of a new direction, and we turn the corner into Act II.

ACT II: The Middle or Body of the Story, pages 25-85

I like to call Act II the Murphy's Law Act. It's where whatever can go wrong ought to, and usually at the worst possible time. Act II should have plenty of unexpected twists and turns, side effects of the action taken by the lead in Plot Point #1. It should challenge the hero, and over its course force him to adapt, to change and grow.

Also, if Act I is the set-up, then the first portion of Act II is what Blake Snyder, author of the screenwriting book _Save the Cat_, called the "fun & games" portion of the script. This is where all sorts of unanticipated consequences result from the action the hero has taken at the end of Act I at that first Plot Point.

The first portion of Act II is also quite often what drew people to the movie, or if you're the writer, it's not uncommonly what made you want to write the script in the first place. It's where you really get to start having fun with what you've set in motion in Act I.

The second act is about the hero pursuing what he wants (his goal), and coming up against and overcoming various obstacles and discovering new opportunities in the course of that pursuit. These include possibly joining forces with others, maybe even previous enemies; learning new information and skills; taking new chances, and behaving in new ways. And, in the course of doing so, becoming/evolving into someone new.

This character evolution is important as it's at the root of what makes a story feel most satisfying. Again, if "a story is a vehicle for character transformation," generally most of that transformation happens in Act II. If your hero is exactly the same person at the end of the story as he was when he started out, it's usually not as emotionally gratifying for an audience.

You can do that, of course, have a lead who doesn't learn or grow or change throughout the story, but that needs to be intentional, as in the case of a tragedy, or it can tend to be as aggravating in stories as it is in real life. You can wind up with the sort of movie that people walk out of thinking, "So, what was the point of *that*?" Generally speaking, we want to see the hero gain some insight; learn something; and improve in some, even very small, regard, even if he gets there kicking and screaming, perhaps especially if he gets there that way.

Goals throughout Act II can change.

In fact, often as a result of the unexpected consequences encountered as a result of the hero's pursuit of his initial goal, his goal does change, as his problem becomes larger and more complicated. Initially, Michael Dorsey just wants a job, but then he falls for his co-worker Julie, encounters all sorts of other personal and professional complications as a result of impersonating a woman, and ultimately has to kill the golden goose that is Dorothy in order to try to win the girl.

There can be stages of goals, as in *Rocky;* qualifying matches. Or goals can even reverse, as in *Toy Story* where first Woody wants to get rid of Buzz, then later wants to save him; or *Apollo 13*, in which first the astronauts' goal is to get to the moon, then they just want to survive and make it back home alive. But whatever the hero is trying to achieve, and why this is so important to him ought to be clear at any given point throughout the story.

Often there is also someone else in the story, the **antagonist** or **villain**, whose job it is to face off against the hero and try to keep him from achieving his goal. (I'll get into more detail on the subject of villains in Chapter 10.) But even if there is not one clear antagonist, per se, there ought to be other characters who collide and conflict with the protagonist, and multiple obstacles throughout which threaten his reaching his goal.

MIDPOINT - The Point Beyond Which All Will Be Different

The Midpoint is a third, but in my opinion slightly vaguer plot point than the Inciting Incident or Plot Point #1 or Plot Point #2 (which comes at the end of the second act). The definitions for it tend to vary. According to the late screenwriting expert Syd Field, it's "an important scene in the middle of the script, often a reversal of fortune or revelation that changes the direction of the story."

Other definitions I've come across include: "Often a change of tactics or change of scenery, or different environment, though certainly not always." Another: "A major reversal of fortune making the main character's task even more difficult. May be a glimpse at the actual resolution of the picture, or its mirror opposite." And finally, "A major turning point, things will be dramatically different from this point onwards."

You can probably see why I don't put quite as much emphasis

on the Midpoint, as it's little like Jello and can be tough to nail down. That said, I think it can be a useful signpost to keep in mind, if for no other reason than it gives you a way to think about breaking up this, your longest act, into more manageable pieces.

Regardless, Act II is about hills and valleys, twists and turns, and the hero's encountering and overcoming unanticipated obstacles. And generally the more obstacles a character faces on the road to achieving his goal, the more invested we become. If it's all just easy, all just a cakewalk, well then, who cares really? Where's the drama or suspense in that? Again, we go to movies to watch people struggle and, more important, to see them rise to the occasion and overcome their life challenges and whatever obstacles lie in the path between them and their desired goal.

So, Act II should be filled with moments of triumph and moments of despair, the greatest of which is Plot Point #2, when all should look lost, and which leads to Act III.

PLOT POINT #2 - Where all looks lost, about page 85

This is typically the lowest point for the hero and the point at which he seems the furthest from his goal. Here, the more unsolvable things appear for him, the better. Now he's *really* tested. Is he going to take his toys and slink home, roll over and die, or is he going to fight the best way he knows how for whatever it is he most wants?

ACT III: The Ending or Resolution, pages 85-110

Act III is where the hero typically rallies from the low of Plot Point #2 and decides he's either going to achieve his goal, or die trying. Michael Arndt, who was a script-reader before he became a screenwriter has said, "The ending is critical. Having been a reader, I can tell you the town is awash in B- to B+ scripts, scripts that ultimately just really don't fully deliver. *The whole movie should be leading toward the ending.*" (italics mine)

The third and final act is the portion of the script in which the hero's pursuit of what he really, really wants becomes a matter of life or death, either literally or figuratively. The going gets even tougher and the hero encounters his biggest test of all. By this point we should understand why, if he does not achieve what it is he thinks he wants, he believes his life will somehow be over. And we should be caught up in wondering whether or not he will attain his goal. Also, the epiphany—the light-bulb moment of insight and new perception for the hero—if there is one, usually happens here.

It's sometimes helpful in third acts/resolutions to think in terms of, "or else?" If your hero doesn't get the thing he's after, if he doesn't achieve his goal, what's really the worst that can happen? Another word for this is **stakes**. What really is at stake? The "or elses" keep the audience engaged and caring, wondering what's going to happen next and how it's all going to turn out.

By the end, or resolution, (where things are *resolved*), you typically want to see your hero:

- Come into his power.

- Gain some self-knowledge.

- Free himself somehow.

By this point, we usually see that the hero has somehow grown and thus is more able to take on the final challenge and seize the reins of his own life, unless you're writing a tragedy, in which case the hero doesn't do any of these things. He doesn't learn, doesn't change, doesn't grow, doesn't come into his power and doesn't free himself. He remains trapped and thus, doomed. Tragic indeed. Again, the fundamental underlying moral to the story being: *What matters most in life is not what happens to us, it's what we do about it.*

Shaking up the structure - stories that are out of order:

I didn't want to close this chapter without mentioning some examples of inventive storytelling which manage to riff on, and selectively and effectively break some of the rules of the standard three act structure. These are stories that are "out of order."

> "A story should have a beginning, a middle and an end, but not necessarily in that order."
>
> ~ Jean-Luc Godard, filmmaker

Some stand out examples include: *500 Days of Summer, The Hangover, Memento, Eternal Sunshine of the Spotless Mind, and Pulp Fiction.* If you examine these scripts carefully, however (with the possible exception of *Pulp Fiction*, which is really three intertwining stories) all of them have a traditional narrative structure which is then rearranged in the telling of the tale.

Each does have a set-up, a middle and a resolution, and a hero (or heroes) with a clear goal, etc. What's so interesting about them is that they take these traditional elements and manage to rearrange them in time and yet still be coherent. This, obviously, is sophisticated storytelling and, if you can pull it off, can really make your work stand out in a crowd. But make no mistake, it's challenging, and I wouldn't recommend trying something this ambitious the first time out.

Finally, as you begin the process of laying out the road map for your own story, it can be helpful to start thinking in terms of the three acts as you watch other movies. See if you can identify them and the major plot points, as well as the character arcs.

HELPFUL TOOL: DO IT IN A LOG LINE; IN A PARAGRAPH; IN A PAGE

Another exercise I recommend to my students is to try to tell your story in a log line, then in a paragraph, and then in a page.

This process of succinctly summarizing the script you intend to write before you write it can be harder than it looks, precisely because it forces you to really figure out and nail down what your story is about before you begin.

Again, I suggest first practicing with a movie or two that you already know well and love. Get the hang of boiling a story down to its essence and recognizing what the critical story beats and elements are. Properly done, these exercises can serve as road maps and save you months, possibly even years, of wandering in the narrative desert or, to mix my metaphors, becoming shipwrecked.

HELPFUL TOOL: PIXAR'S SHORTHAND

A storyboard artist named Emma Coats at Pixar came up with a clever narrative shorthand for helping one identify these structural pieces, and it goes like this:

Once there was a _____. (Your hero.)

Every day, he _____. (His status quo.)

Until one day, _____. (The Inciting Incident)

Because of that, _____. (Multiple entries go here. These effectively include Plot Point #1, and other ensuing complications in Act II.)

1. _____

2. _____

3. _____, etc.

Until finally, _____ . (Plot Point #2, and turn into Act III)

Ever since then, _____ . (Resolution)

Recommended WATCH: If you want to see more on Pixar's story building process, Pixar animator Austin Madison explains it here. **(https://www.youtube.com/watch?v=aLVi0hjNrig)**

So, that's the overview of what goes on, structurally speaking, in most effective and compelling screenplays. In the next chapters we'll take a closer look at each of these three acts and their functions in greater detail.

SCREENPLAY OVERVIEW TAKEAWAYS:

1. A screenplay typically has three acts: A beginning (Act I); a middle (Act II); and an end (Act III).

2. Each act has a specific purpose and, within it, specific and usually critical structural Plot Points, including an Inciting Incident, Plot Point #1 (at end of Act I), and Plot Point #2 (at end of Act II), and possibly a Midpoint right in the middle of the story.

3. Before you go to draft, ideally you'll want to be able to tell your story in a sentence or two (your log line), in a paragraph, and in a page, and to identify each of these three acts and the significant signposts or plot points within them.

4. Your hero ought to have a clearly identified external goal. It's his pursuit of this goal that is the engine of your plot.

5. The stakes should be raised, things should escalate as the story progresses. The threats should get bigger, the obstacles more formidable. And in the end all ought to come down to a literal or figurative matter of life or death for your hero.

6. You want your story to be resolved in the end, not simply peter out or stop.

SCREENPLAY OVERVIEW WORKSHEET:

1. Who, exactly, is your "somebody?" Who is your hero?

2. What is his status quo?

3. What is his dilemma? How has life thrown him a curveball?

4. What is the "something" that he's after? What, specifically, is his goal?

5. What are some of the obstacles he'll come up against in pursuit of that goal?

6. What does he need as a human being? How will he be somehow changed internally by virtue of the experience of the story?

7. What biggest test or ultimate obstacle does he have to overcome?

8. What is really at stake? In what way will his life be over, again literally or figuratively, if he doesn't achieve his goal?

9. See if you can try to communicate the essence of your story in a log line, in a paragraph, and in a page.

Finally, if you don't know the answers to all these questions at this point, please don't worry. The idea here is simply to get *something* down on paper so that you have something to work with, so that you have a place to begin.

STRUCTURALLY SPEAKING: IN-DEPTH ANALYSIS OF THESE ELEMENTS IN ACTION IN TOOTSIE

READ: Tootsie Screenplay
(http://www.screenwrite.in/Screenplays/Tootsie.pdf)

Screenplay by: Larry Gelbart, Murray Schisgal

(Uncredited: Elaine May, Barry Levinson, Robert Garland)

Story by: Larry Gelbart, Don McGuire

Okay, I know.... *Tootsie* is an old movie, and it's been covered to death in screenwriting books and classes. But I do love this film. (It was no mere coincidence that when I sold my original spec script for what became the film *What Women Want*, Daily Variety referred to it at the time as, "A *Tootsie* of the mind." I considered that high praise indeed.)

Anyway, *Tootsie* is also a brilliant example of the principles I'm trying to illustrate here, and it stars and was directed by none other than my former boss, the amazing Sydney Pollack. So, I figure on all these counts, I should be allowed to slide.

Oh, and one more bit of trivia: Though I came on board with Sydney much later than this film, I'm aware that Dustin Hoffman really wanted Sydney to play the part of his agent, as he believed that their real life relationship mirrored the contentious one between Michael Dorsey and his agent.

According to Susan Dworkin in her book, *Making Tootsie: Inside the Classic Film with Dustin Hoffman and Sydney Pollack*, the part of the agent was originally supposed to be played by Dabney Coleman, who wound up playing Julie's (Jessica Lange's) boyfriend. But Dustin really campaigned to get Sydney to play it, even going so far as to send Sydney roses with a card that read, "Please be my agent. Love Dorothy." Dustin insisted that if Dabney Coleman told his character he'd never work again, he might just dismiss him. But if *Sydney Pollack,* with all his formidable authority and intensity, said that to him, *that* would drive him to put on the dress. And fortunately Sydney, despite the fact that he really didn't want to have two jobs on the film, ultimately relented and turned in not only a wonderful movie but also an unforgettable performance.

ACT I - The Set-Up, Inciting Incident & Plot Point #1

The opening montage establishes Dustin Hoffman's main character of Michael Dorsey and his status quo: his job (or lack thereof), his prodigious talent as an actor, his living situation, the thing he wants, which is to work, and his external dilemma that there is no work. It also helps establish his more internal problem as a person and as man, i.e., what he needs to learn in emotional character terms, how he needs to grow.

That's a lot of ground to cover in the first few minutes of the movie. Here's a link to a clip of Pollack discussing this opening and how many things he was trying to do as economically as possible in it.

Recommended WATCH: Sydney Pollack discuss TOOTSIE, setting up Michael Dorsey's character and establishing how he needs to change. **(https://www.youtube.com/watch?v=V80LvSl2FIE)**

These issues are further illustrated in the birthday party scene, which increases the tension on Michael. He's not only an unemployed actor, he's getting older, and he's not particularly happy about any of this. The birthday party sequence also tells us that he's something of a jerk when it comes to women, at least women he's attracted to. He's so self-absorbed and so busy trying to score that he forgets to relate to them as fellow human beings, thus emphasizing what he needs to learn in emotional terms.

The birthday party scene also serves to flesh out the supporting characters, including his friend Sandy, played by Teri Garr, with whom he has a platonic relationship, and his goofball roommate Jeff, played by so brilliantly by Bill Murray.

The **Inciting Incident** here is Michael's learning that Terry Bishop, a rival actor, has gotten a part that Michael coveted. And this news—which comes as a bolt from the blue—literally puts Michael in motion as he runs to confronts his agent about it.

The ensuing scene with his agent serves to further underline Michael's problem, i.e., what he needs to learn: He's such a jerk, he's so difficult, stubborn and demanding that, despite his considerable talent, no one will work with him.

The scene also definitively establishes exactly what Michael wants, that is, his very specific stated goal: He tells his agent he wants to raise $8,000 to do his roommate's play. Notice, there is nothing in here about making a ton of money, becoming a soap star, falling in love, and certainly nothing about becoming a better man. These are not things he sets out to do, not goals he initially sets out to achieve. They're all unexpected consequences, side effects, that happen as a result of his taking the action to get the specific thing he thinks he wants, i.e.: to raise the $8,000 to do his roommate's play.

Plot Point #1:
The pressure builds on Michael, as his agent tells him that not only will no one in New York work with him, no one in Hollywood wants to either. "*No one* will hire you."

"Oh yeah?..." SMASH CUT TO: Michael in the dress. Remember, Plot Point #1 is the action the hero takes to try to solve his immediate problem. Which in this case it does; Michael does land the job, but then all sorts of unexpected consequences ensue in Act II.

The more drastic that Plot Point #1 action is, typically the better. And here's it's such a great cut, from the "Oh yeah?" straight to him in the dress. He auditions for and gets the job, and his problem is seemingly solved: he's got work.

Recommended WATCH: Plot Point #1 in TOOTSIE, where insult is added to injury and Michael is driven to desperate action. **(https://www.youtube.com/watch?v=BnHqiipcw6g)**

We're 25 minutes in. And now Act II begins.

ACT II - Murphy's Law, Unexpected Consequences/ Challenges & Character Evolution

Now we're into the Body of the Story. This is usually where we first get to see what the movie is really about; in this case it's where we first get to see Michael put on the dress and "become" Dorothy.

Act II is about unexpected twists and turns, ups and downs, and the ensuing complications of the Plot Point #1 Action taken by the hero at the end of Act I.

In Act II these complications include:

- Michael meeting and falling for his co-worker Julie

- Julie's father falling for Dorothy

- Dorothy becoming a sensation on the show

- John Van Horn, a co-star, falling for Dorothy

- Julie concluding that Dorothy is a lesbian

Midpoint: I'd say is when Michael takes the trip to the country with Julie to visit her father. It's both a change of environment and rhythm, and plot-wise it's where Michael really falls for Julie in earnest, and also where Julie's dad falls for Dorothy. After this, things will be dramatically different for him.

By the end of Act II, the thing Michael most wants is Julie, but he can't possibly have her as Dorothy. Things reach their lowest point after Julie's father proposes to Dorothy; Michael as Dorothy tries to kiss Julie; Julie tells Dorothy that while she loves her, she can't *love* her and insists Dorothy tell her father the "truth" (that she's a lesbian); and Michael, now feeling he can't go on like this and desperate to end the ruse, goes to his agent and pleads to get out of the deal, but his agent insists that's impossible.

Plot Point #2:

Michael's now reached his lowest point; he feels completely trapped.

ACT III - The Resolution

In order to resolve the situation, Michael decides to take his life by the reins and "out" Dorothy as a man on live TV. He comes clean to everybody, which has the consequence of initially alienating the people he's come to genuinely care for. But he frees himself anyway, he is finally honest, and this ultimately opens the door for a potential future with Julie. As he tells her, "I was a better man as a woman with you than I ever was with a woman as a man." This is his character arc.

So, in the end, Michael ultimately gets both what he wanted—he gets the $8,000 to do his roommate's play—and more importantly, he gets something he needed as a human being, which is a greater sensitivity and appreciation for women and for other people's feelings in general. He's become a better man.

And the very last scene is lovely in that everything is not wrapped up too neatly, yet we're still left with a sense of hope for the two of them together. After Michael runs into Julie on the street, though she's initially cool, we see her gradually start to warm to him, and the two of them walk away together as friends.

CHAPTER SIX

BEGINNINGS: ACT I, OR THE SET-UP

"Action expresses priorities."

~ Mahatma Gandhi

I N CHAPTER FIVE, I DESCRIBED Aristotle's three-act structure on which most films are based. In this and the following two chapters I will analyze each Act in much more depth, uncovering their hidden structures and unique challenges, and thereby illustrating effective ways of building a strong story.

Your first act is the set-up of your story. This is where you introduce your hero, establish his status quo in life, confront him with a problem and, ideally, get him to take some sort of action to deal with it. Before Act I is over, you'll want to establish both what he wants, his external stated goal; and what he needs (to learn).

Act I is also where we typically learn how the hero may have been treated unfairly by the fates; how he may have been dealt a bad hand in life. I'll get into this topic in greater detail in Chapter Nine, on Building Character(s), but for now, it helps if the unfortunate situation the hero finds himself in is not primarily of his own making. Our knowledge regarding a wound or unfair blow a character may have suffered helps build our sympathy for him.

However, it's also important that often the hero is in trouble not only because fate has somehow dealt him a bad hand, but also because he has accepted his situation as unchangeable and out of his control. In this regard, the hero has in some way sold himself short—and thus is **somehow complicit in his circumstance**.

He has not done whatever hard work he needs to in order to become all he could be. In psychological speak, he's not fully self-actualized. He hasn't fulfilled his true full potential as a human being, and in some way needs to grow in order to rise above whatever misfortunes and obstacles life has sent his way. Thus, the story becomes his opportunity to do so as fate forces his hand.

Typically, the thing a character needs as a human being tends to be larger, more emotionally related than the thing he wants, and tends to have something to do with the way he looks at and lives his life. What your hero needs is to quite literally *build his character*. This most often relates to what he needs to learn—about himself and/or about life—which will enable him to be not just somehow better, but freer and more in charge of his own destiny by the time the final credits roll.

What he needs is what informs his character arc, the way in which he is transformed over the course of the story. Remember, movies are about the moment when somebody's life changes, and not just the externals, but when the hero himself changes.

In order for your hero to have somewhere to go, in order for him to actually *have* an arc by the end of the movie, we need to fully understand where it is that he's beginning. So, in Act I, you'll want to establish some internal weakness or shortcoming of his which will in some way be solved or at least improved upon by the end. This flaw is another part of his status quo that is typically established in the early portion of the film.

Status quo examples:
- In *Toy Story*, Woody is the favorite toy and respected leader in a happy house full of toys. His flaw is that he's fine as so long as he's on top, but when he's not, look out.

- In *The 40-Year-Old Virgin*, Andy is a sweet, shy, horny, lonely guy.

- In *Iron Man*, Tony Stark is a cocky, billionaire war profiteer and playboy.

- In *Thelma & Louise*, Thelma and Louise are mild-mannered, ordinary women living lives of quiet desperation.

- In *The King's Speech*, Bertie is a royal who is unable to speak in public without stuttering.

- In *Roman Holiday*, Gregory Peck is a working-stiff reporter eager to return to New York, and the young Princess is living in a gilded cage; her life is not her own.

Then, about ten pages in, *something happens,* something changes. This something is the Inciting Incident.

The Inciting Incident is the curveball the hero didn't see coming, the thing or event that shakes up his world. Another way of looking at the Inciting Incident is to think in terms of *"if only."* If only this (whatever the Inciting Incident is) hadn't happened, then none of the rest of story would have.

Examples of "If Onlys":

- *Toy Story:* If only Buzz Lightyear hadn't shown up and thrown Woody's whole world for a loop.

- *The 40-Year-Old Virgin:* If only Andy hadn't joined the poker game, the guys never would have stumbled onto his secret: that he's a virgin.

- *Argo:* If only the U.S. embassy in Iran hadn't been overrun and most of the diplomats taken hostage.

- *Iron Man:* If only Tony Stark's convoy hadn't been hit and he hadn't been taken captive in Afghanistan.

- *Thelma & Louise:* If only Thelma hadn't met Harlan, the would-be rapist she meets at the country western bar.

- *The King's Speech:* If only Bertie's father, the King, hadn't died, and if only his brother David hadn't met Wallis Simpson.

- *Little Miss Sunshine:* If only the other little girl hadn't been disqualified from the pageant.

- *Roman Holiday:* If only her "minders" hadn't been so controlling and given her that sedative to calm her down and make her sleep.

- *What Women Want:* If only Helen Hunt hadn't shown up and taken the job Mel Gibson thought was supposed to be his.

- *Bridesmaids:* If only Annie's best friend Lillian hadn't gotten engaged.

- *Only You:* If only Damon Bradley hadn't called.

You get the idea. The Inciting Incident is the thing that puts your hero in motion. Here you establish his problem, and the stronger the dilemma created or at least exacerbated by this event, the better. Then tension builds on him throughout the first act, pressuring him to take some sort of action to try to solve his problem and achieve his goal.

The second critical structural element in Act I is Plot Point #1: *"The action the hero takes to solve what he perceives his problem to be, which results in unexpected consequences."*

Note the word "perceives." Michael Dorsey thinks that if only he could get a job, life would be dandy. Woody thinks that if only he could get rid of Buzz, all would be well. Bertie thinks if only he could learn to speak clearly, his worries would be over. What these characters *perceive* their problem to be is usually somewhat limited, while their actual problems, typically in terms of character issues and how they might need to change or grow, run deeper.

Plot Point #1 is the hero's response to the building pressure put on him by the Inciting Incident, and the action he takes is usually immediate, specific and, ideally, somehow bold. And it often does solve the immediate problem at hand: Michael Dorsey *does* get work; Woody *does* get rid of Buzz; Louise *does* stop the rapist. But these actions also then create other unanticipated consequences, or what I call "side effects," which will shortly begin to make themselves apparent in Act II.

Michael Arndt calls this Plot Point #1 action the "unhealthy choice." For example, Woody's healthy choice would have been to graciously accept that he's going to have to share the spotlight with Buzz. Michael Dorsey could have simply gotten some therapy. Louise could have walked away from Harlan once she managed to stop the rape. Thus, typically by trying to solve one problem, the hero somehow winds up creating and having to deal with other, even larger ones. One thing leads to another.

Here's a link to a terrific short video by Arndt on this topic of setting up your story and the hero's making the unhealthy choice in Plot Point #1. I don't agree that in all cases the action the hero takes at the end of Act I is necessarily an unhealthy choice, as Ardnt asserts. (In *Iron Man*, for example, Tony Stark's decision to get the heck out of Afghanistan and the weapons business seems quite the healthy choice). But I think Arndt's is still an interesting and useful take on the subject of Plot Point #1 and on setting your story in motion.

Recommended WATCH: Michael Arndt on setting up your story.
(https://www.youtube.com/watch?v=A6mSdlfpYLU)

> "Between stimulus and response there is a space. In that space is our power to choose our response. In our response lies our growth and our freedom."
>
> ~ Viktor Frankl, Holocaust survivor,
> *Man's Search for Meaning*

Remember, stories teach us that what matters most is not what happens to us, but what we do about it. That's what makes all the difference. In screenwriting terms, that most critical "space" between stimulus and response might be considered the pages between the Inciting Incident and the first Plot Point at the end of Act I, and between the lowest moment that occurs at the end of Act II, or Plot Point #2, and the resolution. This is not to suggest that your hero won't continue to take action and make important choices throughout the story, only that his first choice—that first major turning point at the end of Act I—is usually the biggest one. It's the one that changes everything that follows, the one that changes the trajectory of the hero's life.

Plot Point #1 Examples:

- *Toy Story:* In a fit of pique, Woody schemes to knock Buzz behind Andy's desk using the race car. But things go awry when Buzz sees the car coming, dives for cover and winds up knocking down a bulletin board. This then creates a domino effect of other paraphernalia on the desk, and ultimately sends Buzz sailing out the window. Problem solved (sort of); Woody's gotten rid of Buzz, but now new, even bigger problems have immediately been created.

- *The 40-Year-Old Virgin:* Andy agrees to go out with the guys, which soon leads to all sorts of unanticipated consequences.

- *Argo:* Tony Mendez's outlandish and daring plan for freeing the six Americans hiding in Tehran is approved and he takes off for Hollywood and Iran.

- *Iron Man:* Tony Stark builds the prototype Iron Man suit (he "becomes" Iron Man for the first time) and manages to escape Afghanistan. He comes home determined not only to build a better version but also to stop being a war profiteer and to get out of the weapons business. This doesn't sit well with his business partner, Obadiah Stane, who, unbeknownst to Tony, now sets out to destroy him.

- *Little Miss Sunshine:* The entire family take off together for the beauty pageant. Here again one could argue that this action doesn't necessarily represent an unhealthy choice, but it certainly does lead to unanticipated consequences and create problems for all concerned.

- *Thelma & Louise:* Louise kills Harlan, the would-be rapist, thus obviously stopping him, but now she and Thelma become fugitives on the run.

- *The King's Speech:* Having been humiliated and scorned yet again by his father King George for his stuttering speech, Bertie now begins to work in earnest with therapist Lionel Logue, (also not an unhealthy choice). Although his speech does slowly begin to improve, he soon must confront greater painful personal demons in the course of his therapy.

- *Roman Holiday:* I believe there are two Plot Point #1s here that converge between Joe Bradley and the Princess. In her case, it's when she escapes the palace and shortly thereafter meets Bradley. In his, it's when he discovers who she is and makes the bet with his boss that will enable him to move back to New York, then sets about spending the day with her so that he can write his expose.

- *Sideways:* About-to-be-married Jack arranges a dinner date for him and Miles with Stephanie and Maya, which soon leads to all sorts of complications, including Jack's ultimately getting his face bashed in.

- *Bridesmaids:* Annie agrees to be her best friend's maid of honor, not realizing what she's let herself in for.

- *What Women Want:* In an attempt to get inside women's heads, Mel Gibson's character layers on an absurd number of women's products, then slips, falls into a bathtub and almost electrocutes himself. When he wakes up, he's suddenly hearing women's thoughts and soon discovers he can read their minds.

The Connection Between Plot Point #1 and Your Log Line:

As you may have noticed from the above examples, **Plot Point #1 is often the essence of the log line**. It's quite often the point at which the thing that was the main inspiration for telling your story really kicks into gear.

So if you're struggling with your log line, take a look at your Plot Point #1 and see if it can help you identify the true heart of your story. Conversely, if you feel you've got a solid log line but are struggling with Plot Point #1, check to see if that's a strong enough turning point, if it's where the story is really kicking in.

If your Act I is working effectively, you've set up your story and established your main characters in the first ten pages. Then the Inciting Incident shakes up your hero's status quo, pressure builds on him, and he takes action to try deal with this change or problem in Plot Point #1. This action then generates reactions which spin things into a new direction as we move into the body of the story in Act II.

HELPFUL TOOL: STORY BEATS & BEAT SHEETS

For outlining and laying out their story, some writers use index cards—either actual cards or the virtual digital ones that come with most screenwriting programs—some use a white board, and others use a BEAT SHEET. Some use all three. What writers are most often asked to turn into producers or studios, however, is the beat sheet.

A Beat Sheet is an abbreviated summary of the main story beats of your script. It doesn't include every single scene, but provides an overview of the most important moments in each act and can serve as a road map for your screenplay.

Here's a Beat Sheet I created for Act I of *Toy Story*.

TOY STORY - ACT I Beat Sheet

- OPENING: MEET ANDY, SEE HIS TOYS

  Credits roll as we meet the toys and their owner, a little boy named ANDY, playing with them. Andy's mom tells us that today is Andy's birthday party.

- TOYS COME ALIVE, WOODY IS THE STAR

  Once Andy is out of sight and earshot, we see all toys have lives of their own beyond being his inanimate playthings, and learn that WOODY, the Sheriff, is both Andy's favorite and their leader.

- TOYS WORRY ABOUT BEING REPLACED, SPY ON ANDY'S PARTY

  Woody calls a staff meeting. Toys are all suddenly panicked about being replaced/winding up in the attic. Woody tries to reassure them, to little avail, then placates them by sending an army of toy soldiers downstairs on a reconnaissance mission to spy on the gift opening. During this scene, we also learn the family is going to be moving soon.

- INCITING INCIDENT - BUZZ LIGHTYEAR ARRIVES

  Presents are opened (a lunch box, board game, etc.) and the toys breathe a collective sigh of relief. But there's one more surprise gift. All the kids are excited about it and come screaming upstairs into Andy's bedroom, then vanish just as quickly, leaving Andy's new toy on the bed. The toys peer over the edge and discover a BUZZ LIGHTYEAR, sitting in Woody's spot. (13 mins in).

- BUZZ IMPRESSES OTHER TOYS, ANNOYS WOODY

  We meet Buzz, learn that he believes he's a Space Ranger whose ship has crash-landed here by mistake. All the toys—except Woody—are impressed by his gadgetry and exaggerated sense of self-importance.

- CHALLENGED, BUZZ PROVES HE CAN FLY
  Woody and Buzz argue over whether Buzz is a toy. Buzz insists he's a Space Ranger and that he can fly. Woody insists he isn't, that he's just a toy and that he can't. Buzz demonstrates—and manages to pull off what Woody terms "falling with style." But all the other toys are wowed, and suddenly Woody realizes he's got competition and grows increasingly jealous.

- WOODY'S PLACE IS USURPED BY BUZZ
  Montage of Woody as the pressure on him builds. See him being replaced by Buzz as the new favorite. The decor in Andy's room changes from western to space theme, Buzz sleeps on the bed, Woody's consigned to the toy chest, etc. Woody is very dejected.

- MEET SID, THE EVIL NEXT-DOOR NEIGHBOR, ANTAGONIST
  Buzz is still bent on repairing his spaceship, but Woody has had it. He threatens Buzz, tells him to stay away from Andy; that Andy is "his." This altercation is interrupted when they all hear SID, the bad seed neighbor kid, making a racket. The toys peer fearfully out the window to see Sid torturing a toy, blowing it up with a firecracker, then laughing with sadistic glee. As Bo Peep says, "The sooner they move, the better."

- PLOT POINT #1 - JEALOUS WOODY ACCIDENTALLY KNOCKS BUZZ OUT THE WINDOW
  Mom offers to take Andy to Pizza Planet and tells him he can bring just one toy. Woody overhears and hopes Andy will choose him but fears he might not. He decides to take matters into his own hands and knock Buzz down behind Andy's desk where Andy won't be able to find him. Woody sends the race car toy barreling into an unsuspecting Buzz, but his plan goes awry when Buzz is accidentally sent sailing out the window instead.

  Woody has gotten rid of Buzz all right, but his plan has

gone further than he intended and has created a whole new set of problems. Buzz is now stranded outside down on the ground below, and the other toys suspect Woody of murder.

And now we're off and running into Act II.

ACT I TAKEAWAYS:

1. Act I is where you set up your hero, his status quo, and his main problem(s) in life, both internally and externally. You establish the thing he wants (his goal) and what he needs to learn as a human being, how he needs to grow or change.

2. The first important structural element in Act I is the Inciting Incident, the bolt from the blue that usually occurs around page 10. This is what changes the status quo for the hero. It's what puts him in motion and is the cause for all that follows.

3. The second critical structural element of Act I is Plot Point #1, which occurs at the end of the act and spins your story into Act II. This is the *action* the hero takes to try to solve what he believes his problem to be, which then results in unexpected consequences.

4. A Beat Sheet is a useful and industry-recognized tool for outlining your story. It enables you to create a road map and allows you to get an overview of your story.

ACT I WORKSHEET:

1. Who is your hero?

2. What does he want? Ideally this goal should be something specific and tangible.

3. What does he need to learn? Another way of putting this:

What is his flaw? How does he need to change or to grow in emotional terms and as a human being over the course of the story?

4. What is your Inciting Incident, the bolt from the blue that is the cause for all that follows? Is it something that happens *to* your hero? Does it happen fairly early in the story? (It should occur about 10 pages in).

5. Is the tension increasing on your hero as your first act progresses, usually as a result of the Inciting Incident?

6. What specific *action* does he take at the end of Act I to try to deal with his problem and achieve his goal? In other words, what is your Plot Point #1?

7. How does this action spin your story into a new direction in Act II?

8. Have you created an Act I Beat Sheet to give you a shorthand overview of your story?

STRUCTURALLY SPEAKING: TOY STORY

READ: TOY STORY Screenplay
(http://www.pages.drexel.edu/~ina22/splaylib/Screenplay-Toy_Story.pdf)

Screenplay by: Joss Whedon, Andrew Stanton, Joel Cohen, Alec Sokolow

Story by: John Lasseter, Pete Docter, Andrew Stanton, Joe Ranft

ACT I: The Set-up is 28 minutes long.

The main character is clearly Woody. We glean that he's the leader and Andy's favorite toy from the opening scene. Other supporting players (toys) are also distinctly introduced in the first ten minutes. Status quo is established.

The **Inciting Incident** is the arrival of Buzz Lightyear, which occurs at 13 minutes in (including the credits), pretty much right on target.

Pressure continues to build on Woody throughout Act I as he becomes more and more irritated with, and sidelined by, Buzz, who quickly usurps his place as Andy's favorite toy.

Plot Point #1- 28 minutes

About 15 or so pages, (or minutes), after the Inciting Incident comes Plot Point #1. Fed up, Woody decides to get rid of Buzz and uses the race car toy to try to knock him down behind Andy's desk, but instead accidentally winds up sending him careening out the window.

ACT II: The Body of the Story & Murphy's Law

Remember, the hero's action often does solve the immediate problem. In this case, Woody *does* get rid of Buzz, but he's also created other unanticipated consequences which snowball and become increasingly problematic in Act II. These include:

- Buzz goes flying far farther than Woody intended, and sailing out the window. Oops.

- The other toys accuse Woody of trying to kill Buzz and attack and shun him. He becomes toy non-grata.

- Shortly thereafter, Woody and Buzz wind up in the family car together, get into a fight, and become so consumed by their conflict that they fall out of the car and are left behind at a gas station. Thus they become truly lost toys.

And all of this, all of these unexpected consequences, happen in the span of just six minutes into Act II. The creators of *Toy Story* brilliantly keep the challenges and obstacles coming virtually nonstop.

Here are a few more threats and obstacles our heroes encounter in Act II:

- They wind up at Pizza Planet and are kidnapped and taken home and captive by the antagonist, evil neighbor kid Sid. Not incidentally, this happens almost exactly at the **Midpoint.**

- They're further threatened by Sid's nasty dog, Scud.

- They encounter other seemingly monstrous toys, who—in a great twist—ultimately turn out to be allies.

This movie is a good example of one in which the hero's main goal changes over the course of the story. First, Woody's goal is simply to get rid of Buzz. Then that plan goes awry, so he has to try to undo the damage and winds up ultimately wanting to save Buzz, (and thus himself).

Obstacles increase in Act II; things go from bad to worse. Act II is also about the hero(es) behaving in new ways in order to deal with the increasing challenges they face. It's all about ups and downs, twists and turns.

A few unexpected TWISTS in Act II:

- At Sid's house, they meet the monster toys and are initially frightened and horrified, but then those toys unexpectedly turn out to be heroic and integral to their escape. I love this twist, with its nice, can't-judge-a-book-by-its-cover moral lesson.

- Buzz inadvertently catches a glimpse of a TV commercial and is shocked to discover he really *is* just a toy. This (hilarious) existential crisis completely devastates him, precipitating an emotional breakdown on his part, and thus is disastrous for Woody, who then finds himself trying to console Buzz. He sincerely tells him what's great about him and about being a toy.

Plot Point #2 - All is Lost

This occurs at about 60 minutes in of 77 minute movie. Thus this film has slightly abbreviated Acts II & III, which is not unusual for a kids' movie.

Our heroes hit a lot of low points throughout the story and overcome a lot of obstacles only to encounter more, but to me, the lowest of the low is when Sid straps Buzz to the rocket, and Woody fails in his attempts to convince Buzz to help try to save the two of them.

At this point, it has truly become a matter of life and death, but they're both completely depressed and appear to have given up. Woody says he's nothing compared to Buzz, but even Buzz seems completely demoralized and defeated.

ACT III: The Resolution

The story turns another corner when Buzz has his epiphany and realizes the truth of what Woody's been trying to tell him all

---

along: that it really is a great thing to be a toy and that next door there's a little boy who needs them. He rallies and now he becomes the cheerleader, and Woody is soon onboard as well. They're now working as a team, have managed to bounce back from their lowest point and have a new attitude and a plan. But they aren't out of the woods yet. They still face their biggest test of all.

They have changed over the course of the story and learned to behave in new ways; and now working together. Along with Sid's misfit toys, they start to seize control of events. In this case, they turn the tables on Sid and teach him a lesson as they cleverly escape his clutches.

Once they vanquish Sid, the last half of Act III quite literally speeds along; and ideally, that is what you want as you approach the end of your story. You don't want to be limping to the finish line. It's clear that Woody and Buzz are really buddies now, neither willing to leave the other behind. The inventiveness and kinetics of their final dash for the moving van are wild and fun, as is the callback of Buzz's ability to "fall with style." And of course the ending is a happy one as they finally triumphantly make their way back into the family mini-van and are reunited with Andy.

Coda/Denouement: The punchline of Christmas and the arrival of a puppy.

CHAPTER SEVEN

MIDDLES: ACT II, OR MURPHY'S LAW

> *"The obstacles are the path."*
>
> ~ Zen proverb

A CT II, THE LONGEST ACT, is the body of your story. After setting up your characters and story in Act I, and before paying things off and winding them up in Act III, you get to play a little with what you've created. Act II is also where the universe will make your hero prove how badly he wants whatever it is that he wants. It will *test* him. And unforeseen consequences and obstacles will ideally have the effect of forcing him to grow and to start behaving in new ways.

Plot Point #1 is the gateway to Act II, and the first half of Act II is usually the point at which the movie turns in something of a new direction and also really starts to kick into high gear. You've come to what is often the main reason you wanted to write a particular story in the first place and the main thing the audience has paid to see.

Examples of beginnings of Act II:

- In *Tootsie*, as discussed, it's where Dustin Hoffman first puts on the dress.

- In *Toy Story*, it's where the toys first find themselves out in the big, bad world alone.

- In *The 40-Year-Old Virgin*, it's where Andy first leaves his comfort zone, ventures into the dating world and begins to interact with women.

- In *Argo*, it's where Tony Mendez heads to Hollywood to put his phony movie/escape plan into action.

- In *Iron Man*, it's where Tony Stark becomes "Iron Man," first flies in the prototype suit, then returns home and announces he wants out of the weapons trade and sets about building an even more elaborate version.

- In *Little Miss Sunshine*, it's where the whole family piles into the van and hits the road together.

- In *Thelma & Louise*, it's where Thelma and Louise go from mild-mannered, law-abiding women to outlaws on the run.

- In *The King's Speech*, it's where Bertie begins to work with Lionel in earnest to try to overcome his speech problems.

- In *Roman Holiday*, it's where the princess heads out on her own into the festive night streets of Rome, and then meets and goes home with reporter Joe Bradley.

- In *Sideways*, it's where Jack and Miles go on a dinner date with Stephanie and Maya.

- In *What Women Want*, it's where Mel Gibson first discovers he can read women's minds and starts to realize what that means.

- In *Only You*, it's where Faith first finds herself in Italy.

Act II is also where the complications and ramifications of the action the hero took at the end of Act I, i.e., Plot Point #1, really start to manifest. As you can see, the moral to Act II for the hero is often a case of "Be careful what you wish for," as the unexpected consequences of his action at the end of Act I begin to mount.

Once Plot Point #1 happens, it's important that your hero has crossed the Rubicon. It's a new world, and whatever he's done can't be easily undone, if it can be undone at all. The harder it is for him to escape the consequences of the action he took at the end of Act I, and the more sudden, extreme and instantaneous the consequences, generally the stronger your story will be.

Ideally, this action creates an immediate and dramatic change in the hero's circumstances. Things can and usually do get increasingly complicated from here, but regardless, the initial change in his circumstances ought to be immediate and significant.

One good way to approach writing your second act is to dream up all that can possibly go wrong for your hero, and then brainstorm some inventive ways for him to deal with and overcome these obstacles, ways that will ultimately enable him to grow as a human being.

All of that having been said, Act II can become a slog from a writer's standpoint, and too often from an audience's. In writing Act I, you've usually got creative momentum working for you. You're excited to begin telling your story. By the time you're waist-deep in Act II, however, that momentum and excitement can start to wane and morph into what feels like an endless swamp of story problems.

Act II can turn into a forced march and can too easily fall into the trap of feeling episodic and meandering, thus losing narrative momentum. It takes focus and discipline to keep it on track. If you find the energy and momentum starting to flag, here are a couple of important points you'll want to keep in mind about Act II:

1. ACT II is where Murphy's Law really kicks in; it's about twists and turns; ups and downs.

ACT II is all about unexpected consequences and unforeseen obstacles and how the hero finds clever ways to overcome them. It's about setbacks, but it's also about the hero making progress in spite of them, both toward his goal, and in terms of his personal evolution.

This is where the principle of cause and effect really comes into play. If you happen to remember that old kids' game Mouse Trap, in which everything in the game was one great big chain reaction, you'll have a good mental image mnemonic for Act II.

Act II is your Mouse Trap act: Because your hero takes one action, something else, usually unexpected or unanticipated, results. It's where things do *not* go like clockwork. You want to keep the complications coming for him, keep the challenges building one on upon another. There is progress, but it isn't easy, it takes hard work. There are moments of triumph and moments of despair, and it's often a matter of two steps forward, one step back.

HELPFUL TOOL: "and therefore" or "but"
Trey Parker and Matt Stone, creators of *South Park* and *Book of Mormon*, maintain that if between the beats of your story you can add the words "and then," you're on the wrong track and that what you've written is potentially inherently boring. Instead, they suggest that you want to be able to add either the words "and therefore" or the word "but" between each story beat. In other words, *each scene causes or is complicated by the following one.* That's what truly makes a story.

Watch them explain this scene connection principle to a screenwriting class at New York University. It's all well worth watching, and is only six minutes long, but if you want to skip to the critical portion, start at 3:50.

Recommended WATCH: Trey Parker & Matt Stone at NYU
(http://www.mtvu.com/shows/stand-in/trey-parker-matt-stone-surprise-nyu-class/)

Remember: This happens, *and therefore* that happens; that happens, *but* then this happens. Try writing short descriptions of your scenes out, putting these words between your main story beats, and see if you can create a strong cause and effect chain of events. It will help to keep your story moving powerfully forward and create anticipation in your audience.

2. ACT II is also about character evolution.

As new complications and obstacles arise, your hero has to develop new skills, gain knowledge and change some of his previous behavior in order to contend with them.

For example, over the course of Act II, Michael Dorsey gains a greater appreciation for women as people and for other people's feelings in general; Woody and Buzz grudgingly come to appreciate each other so that by Act III they're able to work as a team; Thelma learns how to wield a gun and rob a liquor store, etc. And as they learn, the heroes change and grow as human beings. Little by little, they evolve somehow, and how they change throughout the movie is their character arc.

Remember, "Movies are about the moment when somebody's life changed." They're really about the "moments," plural, but the time frame of a film usually covers a relatively small fraction of the life of the hero. It's this critical passage that interests us, the one in which someone was forced to rise to the occasion and managed or failed to do so. We like to witness and vicariously experience the life-changing experience.

Maybe part of the reason this element of stories provides us with such pleasure is that we don't see it all that often in real life. Patterns can be hard to break. For better or worse, most people tend to remain pretty much the same from year to year. If they were honest, they remain honest. If they were liars, they're usually still playing fast and loose with the truth twenty years later. But we all want to *believe*. It's tremendously heartening and inspiring to watch someone somehow get "better," to fight hard to achieve something and thereby live a fuller, freer, more authentic life.

It is over the course of Act II that the hero changes, so that by ACT III, when he faces his biggest challenge of all, he is somehow transformed and thereby more able to take it on and overcome.

BREAKDOWN OF ACT II:

First half of Act II, roughly pages 25-50
This is the fun and games portion of the script and is quite often the crux of the original inspiration for the movie. After the set-up of Act I, the story really kicks into high gear here at the beginning of Act II. It's a place for you to play and really revel in your premise.

Midpoint, about page 50, or halfway into the script
As previously mentioned, there are a number of definitions for the Midpoint out there. My favorite is the simplest, if also the broadest: *"A major turning point, things will be dramatically different from this point onward."*

Midpoint Examples:
- *The 40-Year-Old Virgin:* It's when Trish shows up in the electronics store, and Andy, having gained some confidence from his new friends, actually manages to flirt with her and ask her out.

- *Argo:* When Tony Mendez gets the green light to go to Tehran and move forward with his rescue mission.

- *Iron Man:* When Tony Stark puts on the prototype Iron Man suit, battles the bad guys and escapes Afghanistan by taking flight for the first time.

- *Little Miss Sunshine:* When Grandpa dies.

- *Thelma & Louise:* When they discover that Brad Pitt's character, J.D., has stolen their money. This event is the main catalyst for Thelma's character arc. Louise is devastated, and it's here that Thelma begins to take charge.

- *The King's Speech:* When Bertie opens up in Lionel's office and makes his real breakthrough in connecting his speech problems with the abuse he suffered as a child.

- *Only You:* When Faith (Marisa Tomei) meets Robert Downey Jr. who claims he's "Damon Bradley," ostensibly the man of her dreams.

Second half of Act II (after the Midpoint), roughly pages 50-75

You want to keep the threats and obstacles coming here, and keep making your hero find new and inventive ways to overcome them. Problems should mount, stakes get higher, pressure increases, threats and complications multiply, so that by the end of Act II, by Plot Point #2, the last bit of hope for your hero *seems* dashed.

Plot Point #2, The lowest point, about page 75-80

As Act II comes to a close the pressure on the hero gets cranked up to its highest level yet. The obstacles, threats and complications increase to the point that the hero seems furthest from his goal, and all looks lost.

Plot Point #2 Examples:

- In *The 40-Year-Old Virgin:* Andy refuses to have sex with Trish and she confronts him, discovers his porn collection and his weird vagina sculptures (from the birth control meeting), and concludes he's at best a closet weirdo and possibly a serial killer.

- In *Argo:* Tony Mendez's boss tells him to call off the mission.

- In *Iron Man:* Obadiah manages to paralyze Tony Stark, steals his Iron Man technology, and then announces he's going to kill Pepper Potts.

- In *Thelma & Louise:* Harvey Keitel's sympathetic lawman tells them he's got no choice but to charge the two women with murder, and the police are closing in.

- In *The King's Speech:* After having made some real progress together, Lionel suggests that Bertie could make a better king than his brother and, as a result, they have a falling out and stop speaking.

- In *Roman Holiday*: The secret service agents come to try to drag the princess back to the palace, and although she and Joe Bradley barely manage to escape them, they recognize their time together is almost up.

- In *Sideways:* Miles loses Maya for having lied to her, then finds out his book hasn't sold because the publisher can't figure out how to market it and his agent is giving up. And Jack gets his nose broken by Stephanie.

As you can see, things tend to get *really* bad in Plot Point #2, and the worse they get for your hero, generally the more invested an audience will be in seeing how it all turns out.

OTHER WAYS TO KEEP THINGS MOVING IN ACT II:

So, Act II is about unforeseen complications and mounting obstacles, ups and downs, twists and turns, and characters having to evolve, learn new skills and behave in new ways. Still, sometimes it can be hard to keep Act II moving. Here are a couple more tricks for maintaining momentum in this longest act:

SET AN ALARM: Build in some sort of ticking clock, a definite deadline by which the hero must achieve his goal. *Little Miss Sunshine, Speed, The Hangover, Die Hard,* and a slew of other successful films use this device. A ticking clock creates greater dramatic tension and suspense for an audience as it puts even more pressure on the hero. Not only does he have to achieve his goal, he's got a hard deadline by which he must do so, and that clock is ticking throughout.

HIT THE ROAD: Put your characters on a road trip of some sort, thereby creating an inherent sense of forward momentum and progression toward a specific goal. *Little Miss Sunshine*, incidentally, uses both a ticking clock and a road trip.

Remember, the key to Act II is that you want your story to build and keep moving forward as the script progresses, not simply to be a series of random episodes and events piled one upon another. Keep building that cause and effect chain of action and reaction and let your hero grow, even if in fits and starts.

ACT II TAKEAWAYS:

1. Act II is where Murphy's Law really kicks in. Whatever can go wrong, should, and usually at the worst possible time. It's where one thing leads to another and the hero gets in ever deeper.

2. Act II is about obstacles, complications and side effects of the hero's action in Plot Point #1.

3. In terms of character, Act II is about evolution. Your hero will ideally evolve and grow over the course of it, so that by the time we get to Act III he is somehow a changed person. He will have learned something new by virtue of his trials and will be able to behave in new ways in Act III.

4. There is often a Midpoint in this act, and thus the middle of the story, after which nothing will be the same.

5. Act II ends with Plot Point #2, the lowest point, where the hero seems furthest from his goal and appears completely outmatched by villains and circumstances.

ACT II WORKSHEET:

1. Has your story headed in a new direction as a result of the action your hero takes at the end of the Act I?

2. At the beginning of Act II, has your hero somehow crossed the Rubicon? Is there now no going back?

3. In the first half of Act II, are you milking your premise for all it's worth? Has the driving inspiration for writing your story really kicked in and are you having fun and games?

4. At the Midpoint, does something happen that will make things significantly different from here on out?

5. Are the obstacles mounting as the act progresses? Are there plenty of ups and downs, twists and turns, obstacles encountered, and moments of triumph and despair?

6. Is your hero evolving? Is he developing in himself qualities he didn't know were there?

7. Does all look lost for him at the end of Act II, i.e., at Plot Point #2? The goal here is to make this lowest point feel organic to the story and its characters, not artificial or contrived.

8. Does your hero have to give up anything by the end of Act II in order to achieve his goal and free himself in the resolution?

9. Can you insert either "and therefore" or "but" between your main story beats?

10. Have you created an Act II Beat Sheet to give yourself an overview of your story to this point?

STRUCTURALLY SPEAKING: THE 40-YEAR-OLD VIRGIN

READ: THE 40-YEAR-OLD VIRGIN Screenplay
(http://screenplayexplorer.com/wp-content/scripts/40-yearold-virgin.pdf)

Written by: Judd Apatow and Steve Carell

I like to include this movie in my teaching not only because I think it's quite well-structured and has a solid character arc, but also because, tonally, this is where the romantic comedy has gone, for better or worse, in the last ten years or so.

Judd Apatow and his imitators and protégées now pretty much own this genre, and movies like this—*Superbad, Forgetting Sarah Marshall, Bridesmaids, Trainwreck,* etc.—movies that are far cruder and coarser than the romcoms of old—are now kind of the standard. There are, of course, always exceptions—*500 Days of Summer* comes to mind—but the changing standards and landscape are something to bear in mind if your goal is to write romantic comedy.

Act I

The first 10 minutes of this movie establish quite a bit about the main character, Andy. Even before the credits end, we know his status quo. His world is in equilibrium, even if it's not exactly great. He lives alone; he's orderly; he's a good cook; he's a something of an arrested adolescent geek; he's a sweet guy; he's horny; and he's sort of pitiful.

This is all done economically and visually, there's not a lot of dialogue in the opening minutes of the film except for the rather hit-you-over-the head bit from his neighbors which pretty much lays out exactly what the movie is about: "That guy needs to get laid."

Regardless, we make an almost immediate emotional connection with Andy, he's almost instantly sympathetic. How exactly does this happen? Well, first, in true *Save the Cat* fashion, he's shown to be a nice guy. He's sweet to his neighbors, he's polite and well-intentioned. And once at the electronics store where he works, it's quickly clear that he's probably the most fundamentally decent and respectful guy there. But he's shy and, we later learn, he's been treated unfairly by the fates. He's been unlucky in love and sex; as a result, he has sold himself short in life. He has pretty much resigned himself to this lonely, stunted life.

The Inciting Incident: At 13 minutes in is the poker game, at which, despite his best efforts to conceal the fact, Andy's co-workers discover that he's a virgin. The bolt from the blue is that suddenly his secret is out.

The pressure builds on him from that point. He's increasingly humiliated and harassed by his co-workers about his virginity and thus finally takes action to try to solve his problem at the end of Act I.

Notice how well orchestrated the other supporting characters are. Paul Rudd's character, David, is a true romantic, if somewhat stalker-ish. Jay is a sexist player and jerk, but, in spite of it, he's still likable, and he too is ultimately redeemed. Mooj, the Indian guy, is ridiculously foul-mouthed and seemingly oblivious to the fact that the things he says tend to be jaw-droopingly crude, and yet at the same time there's a sweet sincerity about him.

Plot Point #1, 23 minutes

Their peer pressure leads to Plot Point #1, the action Andy takes to solve his problem: He goes out to a bar with the guys for the first time in an effort to finally get laid. There he does actually meet an attractive girl (well-played by Leslie Mann); she's into him and invites him to take her home. He's almost there, but then she turns out to be a complete nutcase alcoholic (unanticipated consequences) and the evening suddenly turns into Mr. Toad's Wild Ride, with lots of literal twists and turns, leaving him just hoping to make it home alive.

And now we're fully into Act II.

Act II: Murphy's Law & Character Evolution

Some unexpected obstacles or challenges Andy encounters in Act II:

- The Mr. Toad's Wild Ride with a drunk Leslie Mann

- The excruciating waxing session, (which, to hear the filmmakers tell it, was real)

- The date with a transvestite hooker

- Meeting and dealing with Trish's kids

But Act II is not only about obstacles, it's also about the overcoming of them; about moments of triumph along the way. Andy starts to grow over the course of it, and we see him, little by little, changing, growing, becoming more confident and more comfortable in his own skin. Along these lines, he:

- Comes out of his shell at work

- Flirts with the bookstore girl

- Gets promoted to the selling floor

- Bonds with the guys

- Most important, he meets Trish and they agree to go out, the **Midpoint.**

- Develops a relationship with her and her kids

He also:

- Becomes best salesman, and is promoted to floor manager

- Consoles Jay

- Takes Trish's daughter to get birth control pills

- Takes a driving lesson

- Gets a moped (it's not a car, but it's a step)

Remember, character evolution is not a steady, unbroken upward trajectory; that wouldn't be dramatically interesting. It's not suddenly all smooth sailing, but more jagged, up and down, two steps forward, one step back. But overall Andy is definitely moving forward, until...

Plot Point #2 - The lowest point
When Trish forces the sex issue, he's unwilling to go through with it or to tell her the truth. They fight over his toys, she wonders if he's not some sort of genuine weirdo/serial killer and they break up.

Act III - The Resolution - Character Arc completed
Now Act III answers question raised in Act I: Will Andy ever get laid? But he wants more now. At the beginning of Act III he gives up the opportunity to have sex with the bookstore girl and goes after Trish, the woman he loves.

Equally important, we're wondering if Andy will ever grow up? Will he get what he needs in emotional, self-actualization terms? In order to do this, he faces his biggest test of all, which is to come clean with Trish about who he really is. He has to own his virginity, share that secret with her, and that intimacy allows her to fall back in love with him and allows them to finally consummate their relationship.

Regarding the end of the movie, Garry Shandling, (whose Larry Sanders show Apatow once worked on), advised Apatow that for Andy, sex with Trish had to be seen as not just good, not even just great, but as the most amazing thing *ever*. Hence the hilariously silly, slightly surreal and giddy over-the-top "Age of Aquarius" dance sequence at the very end of the film, which tonally strikes just the right note and not incidentally also serves to reunite everyone in the story.

Remember, by the end, you want to see your hero:

- Come into his power

- Gain some self-knowledge

- Free himself somehow

- Take the reins of his life

If movies are about the moment where somebody's life changed, where they grow somehow over the course of the story, I think this one is an excellent example.

CHAPTER EIGHT

ACT III: ENDINGS, OR ELSE...

> *"Just write the ending. That way, technically, you're finished, then you can go back and just fill in the missing parts."*
>
> ~ Judd Apatow to Jason Reitman, who asked him for advice when Reitman found himself stuck trying to finish *Up in the Air*

J ASON REITMAN, WRITER/DIRECTOR WHO CO-WROTE *Up in the Air*, has said it took him five years to write that script and that even after all that time, he found himself struggling to complete it. At the time, he ran into his friend Judd Apatow at the Santa Barbara International Film Festival, confided that he was stuck and asked if Judd had any recommendations. Apatow gave him the advice above. Reitman claims that this suggestion, which might sound a little flippant, was in fact very helpful. And I can see why, for a couple of reasons:

First, psychologically, Apatow is right. If it takes playing a few mind games with yourself in order to get to that finish line, then so be it. Trick yourself into completing the thing. Second, and more important, you really do want to know how your story ends before you get there. The ending is critical, it's where everything that came before ought to have been leading, and it can be surprisingly difficult to nail down.

Your ending is also, inevitably, the moral to your story. Screenwriting guru Robert McKee says it's where, thematically speaking, you're making a statement about what is the "right" way to live, whether you consciously mean to or not.

Given the importance of the ending, you would be amazed how many scripts don't so much end as simply stop, as though they've been mercifully put out of their misery. It's sad to see how many don't build to any discernible climax that is resolved in any satisfying way, but instead peter out. These stories end not with an emotional bang but with what feels like an arbitrary whimper. You don't want yours to be one of those.

KNOW THY ENDING

Naturally, things can and will change and evolve over the course of writing your screenplay, but I can't emphasize this enough: Know thy ending. You need to know where you're headed, and why, in order to stand any chance of arriving there. You don't want to kid yourself that you'll just start writing and then figure it out when you get there. That's a recipe for throwing out lots of carefully crafted scenes and dialogue, winding up with many bald spots from all the hair you'll tear out, and spending five years writing a script. (And that's if you're Jason Reitman and have already had a significant amount of practice at this.)

In a January 2016 interview with Richard Stayton for the Writers Guild magazine, *Written By*, Woody Allen said:

> *"I always found it was a mistake not to know the ending in advance because one of the common traps that writers fall into—and I fell into many times when I started—you get a great initial idea that doesn't go anyplace and then you have no story and you find you've written 20 or 50 pages or 70 pages and you're out, you're gone. All the work you put in doesn't mean anything. You have nowhere to go with the story.*
>
> *"So it's very important to have the end when you start, not to go into it unless you know. You cannot have the beginning and you cannot have some of the middle and*

figure, 'Well, it will come as I develop.' You must have the ending. It's critical."

STAKES

If Act II is the Murphy's Law act, then Act III is about DO OR DIE. It's also about completing character arcs, and it's where everything is, of course, ultimately resolved. But before that happens, it's where things usually boil down to a figurative or literal matter of life or death for the hero and is about what is truly at stake.

You want the stakes to be high and clear. Act III is about the "or else." Your hero is going to achieve his goal, or else what? How bad will life really be for him if he fails? The answer is, it ought to be pretty damn bad. It ought to *matter*.

Examples of "or else's"/Stakes:

- In *Tootsie*, is Michael Dorsey going to be able to get rid of Dorothy and win Julie's heart?

- In *Toy Story*, are Woody and Buzz ever going to escape evil Sid's clutches and find their way back home to Andy?

- In *The 40-Year-Old Virgin*, is Andy ever going to manage to win Trish back and lose his virginity?

- In *Argo*, is Tony Mendez going to be able to smuggle the diplomats out of Iran alive?

- In *Iron Man*, is Tony Stark going to be able to stop Obadiah from killing Pepper and using his technology to wreak worldwide havoc?

- In *Little Miss Sunshine*, is Olive going to be able to compete and win the pageant?

- In *Thelma & Louise*, are they going to be able to evade the long arm of the law and make their getaway to Mexico?

- In *The King's Speech,* is Bertie going to be able to speak well in public and thus be able to fulfill his role as leader and king?

- In *Roman Holiday*, is the princess going to walk away from her role with the monarchy or give up what may be the love of her life?

Again, Act III is kicked off by Plot Point #2, where all seems lost. After that low point there is usually a moment of clarity, a moment of resolve on the part of the hero. He takes full stock of his faculties and the situation and decides he's not giving up. He redoubles his efforts, somehow turns the page, and now there is no turning back. From here he heads down the road of Act III toward his greatest overall global goal and the end of the story.

For example, at the end of Act II and beginning of Act III of *Toy Story*, Woody and Buzz finally manage to escape from Sid (Act II goal achieved), but their global goal, reuniting with Andy, remains out of reach. In fact, there is often a setback in regard to the global goal. Now things get *really* tough, but now our hero or heroes, having gone through ACT II and fought and learned and grown and changed, are up to the challenge.

CHARACTER ARCS

Act III is where we really see how the hero has (or in some cases, has not) been transformed. It's where we see his character "arc."

The character arc underpins what makes a story satisfying and gives it emotional resonance. The significance of this element speaks to our collective desire to believe that the struggles we all go through are not for nothing. We want to believe that people—that *we*—can improve, learn, grow and thereby ultimately triumph over our life's obstacles, misfortunes and mistakes. To see that a hero can change and live a fuller life makes us feel that that we, too, can change for the better.

Not only do we want to see our heroes get what they want, we want to feel that they *deserve* it. It's important that an audience feel convinced that the hero has earned whatever it is he was seeking by virtue of his hard work, sacrifice, courage and of having in some way become a better, more authentic, more self-actualized person.

Examples of Obstacles Catalyzing and Forcing Character Arcs:

*   *Tootsie*

    Michael Dorsey is a bit of a jerk when the movie begins, particularly when it comes to his relationships with women. He's self-involved and all about the score, not really relating to women as human beings. Then he "becomes" one in order to survive as an actor, and suddenly he is forced into experiencing the struggles women face on a daily basis. He gains insight into their lives and a new appreciation for them.

    By the end, he has become a better, more empathetic person, someone who can relate to the opposite sex in a more sincere way. He grows to feel guilty about deceiving those close to him, particularly Julie and her Dad. It is this feeling for others that ultimately leads him to drop the charade and thus opens the door to the possibility of a real relationship with Julie.

*   *Toy Story*

    Woody is generally a good guy but becomes temperamental when he's forced to share the spotlight with the new toy in town, Buzz Lightyear. When, as a result of his own jealous actions gone awry, he and Buzz find themselves out in the big, bad world together, he must gain humility, befriend and learn how to work with Buzz in order to survive.

    They're both changed by their adventure, so that by the time we move into Act III, they're pals, a team. Buzz accepts and makes peace with the fact that he's a toy, and Woody accepts and makes peace with Buzz. This is truly a buddy movie, and each main character has an arc.

- *The 40-Year-Old Virgin*
  When the story opens, Andy is a sweet, shy, nerdy, lonely guy who has resigned himself to a life without love (or sex). When the guys he works with discover his secret, their pressure forces him to finally deal with his problem, and when he meets Trish, the woman he falls for, he's forced to grow up. He is finally freed when he admits to Trish that he's a virgin. No longer living a lie, his making this revelation allows for a genuinely intimate relationship with her.

- *Iron Man*
  At the beginning, Tony Stark is a cocky, uber-wealthy war profiteer. After being taken hostage in Afghanistan and there meeting a doctor who saves his life, he builds the prototype Iron Man suit, manages to escape and returns home determined to use his skills differently to benefit humanity. He realizes that he wants to do more than sell weapons to destroy the world; instead he wants to try to save it. He also recognizes that he wants something more in his personal life than a string of one-night stands and begins to acknowledge his genuine feelings for his loyal assistant and friend, Pepper.

- *Argo*
  We're to understand that Tony Mendez's experience in Iran has transformed him and led him back to his estranged wife. Um, okay. I think this one is a bit of a stretch, honestly, and one of the only weak links in this film, but we'll play along.

- *Little Miss Sunshine*
  Olive doesn't win the pageant (one assumes), but the family all get something even better. The struggles they've faced and overcome together in the process of

getting her there allow them to grow closer. In the end, everyone rallies behind her, connecting and having fun together.

- *Thelma & Louise*

  When the movie opens, they are two mild-mannered women living what one might call lives of quiet desperation. But after Thelma is almost raped and Louise shoots and kills the rapist, they're forced to run for their lives. In the process, they both come alive and reclaim their power. Thelma comes into her own and takes charge once she and Louise are told that they're going to be arrested for murder. She becomes, to paraphrase the poet, "the master of her fate ... the captain of her soul."

- *The King's Speech*

  Bertie, the Duke of York, has lived with a stuttering speech impediment all his life. He's forced to rise to the occasion and finally try to deal with it and its underlying cause as a result of the combined challenges of the death of his aging father and his brother's abdication, not to mention the outbreak of World War II. As a result, he ultimately must come to terms with the pain of his childhood and this makes him not only a better speaker and king, but also a less guarded, more openly empathetic and appreciative man.

ACT III ANSWERS THE QUESTION POSED IN ACT I

If Act I establishes that the hero wants something badly and goes after it against all odds, then Act III answers the question: Does he get it?

Act I raises the question, and Act III answers it; the two are connected, or at least they ought to be. You want your resolution to fulfill the promise of the premise that is set up in Act I. What have we been wondering about all along? What's the whole movie been leading to? In Act III, you pay off the set-up.

Examples of questions raised by Plot Point #1:

- In *Tootsie*, will Michael Dorsey ever find work and be able to put on his roommate's play?

- In *Toy Story*, will Woody manage to get rid of Buzz?

- In *The 40-Year-Old Virgin*, will Andy lose his virginity?

- In *Argo*, will Tony Mendez be able to free the diplomats and make it out of the country alive?

- In *Iron Man*, will Tony Stark be able to become Iron Man and defeat the war-mongering bad guys?

- In *Little Miss Sunshine*, will Olive win the pageant?

- In *Thelma & Louise*, will Thelma and Louise get away with murder?

- In *The King's Speech*, will Bertie be able to speak in public?

- In *Roman Holiday*, will the princess abandon her royal duties forever in favor of the freedom and love she may have found in civilian life?

- In *Sideways*, will Miles manage to win over Maya?

THE BIGGEST OBSTACLE FOR THE HERO
COMES RIGHT BEFORE THE END:

After the low of Plot Point #2, as we begin Act III, there is a turnaround. The hero digs deep and summons his courage. He decides he is no longer going to live at the mercy of the fates and/or the villain; he is going to live on his terms.

This is where your hero faces his biggest test of all. Although the hero rallies, coming back from the low of Plot Point #2 and manages to win the battle, the war is not yet over. Usually he faces his biggest obstacle of all in Act III. Now he uses everything he's learned over the course of the story and, come hell or high water, he will not be denied. There is still one great big push required if he's to achieve his global goal.

Examples of Biggest Obstacles to the Global Goal:

- *Tootsie:* Michael Dorsey has called off the ruse; he has "killed" Dorothy and effectively confessed his deception to the world and to the girl he loves (and her father). He's free of the job and of living the lie—which is what he wanted (battle won)—but now everyone hates him, especially Julie and her dad.

- *Toy Story:* Woody and Buzz manage to escape from evil Sid (battle won), but now the moving truck with the family in it has pulled away without them.

- *The 40-Year-Old Virgin:* It appeared that Andy had won Trish's heart and they'd successfully made it to the 20 date mark (battle won), but now by refusing to have sex with her, he's completely driven her away. In fact, she now suspects he may be a serial killer.

- *Argo:* Tony Mendez has decided to go through with his plan (battle won), but now has to somehow lead the hostages through the gauntlet of getting to the airport, past dozens of Iranian guards, and safely onto the plane and out of the country.

- *Iron Man:* Tony Stark rallies after being paralyzed by Obadiah (battle won), but still has to battle *mano a mano* against him as his enemy is now sporting an enormous Iron Man suit that dwarfs Tony's.

- *Little Miss Sunshine:* The family just barely makes it to California and the pageant in time for Olive to compete, (battle won), but now everyone realizes what she's really up against and how ill-suited she actually is for this thing.

- *Thelma & Louise:* They actually don't really achieve their Act II goal, which is to escape the law. In fact, at this point the law finally fully catches up to them (battle lost). And shortly thereafter they choose to give up the ultimate thing—their lives. And yet, in the end, despite being surrounded by overwhelming police power, they manage to free themselves. I'd say war won.

- *Roman Holiday:* The princess and Joe Bradley manage to escape the agents sent to drag her back to the palace (battle won), but now she must decide whether to return to royal life, and he has to choose whether to publish the story outing her or give up winning his bet with his editor and his chance to return to New York City.

AGAINST ALL ODDS

Another element to consider in this "biggest test" is that if you're writing a movie in which there is one clear antagonist or villain, the ending should pit your hero directly against that enemy and your hero ought to seem vastly outmatched. It should feel like David versus Goliath.

In *Argo*, Tony Mendez and his little group go up against what seems like the entire Iranian guard. In *Iron Man*, Tony Stark's Iron Man suit is dwarfed by Obadiah's. Another great example of this principle is the film *Aliens*, in which Sigourney Weaver must go up against what is quite literally the *mother* of all aliens. That scene is a good one to keep in mind when imagining your Act III final battle versus an all-powerful antagonist.

In order to achieve this second act goal, in order to win the battle and turn the corner into Act III, the hero usually gives up something or changes for the better.

Act III is the place where the hero fully arcs, where the way he has changed or grown over the course of the story is fully demonstrated. But remember, becoming something of a new person is not usually his stated goal. It's not what he explicitly set out to do; it's what he inadvertently winds up doing; it's how he winds up evolving because the situation demands it. And usually the hero *must* change in some fundamental way in order to get whatever he most wants, in order to achieve his goal.

You can see how what the hero gives up is often intertwined with his personal evolution; it's often connected both to his achievement of his global goal and to his gaining the character growth he needs.

Examples of Things Given Up:

- *Tootsie:* Michael Dorsey gives up the lie (and the fame and the paycheck) of being Dorothy.

- *Toy Story:* Woody gives up trying to best Buzz and Buzz gives up his illusions of being a Space Ranger. In Act III, instead of just bumbling along, bickering and reacting to the threats they face, they join forces. As a team they manage to achieve their goal.

- *The 40-Year-Old Virgin:* Andy gives up denying who he really is and thus is able to win the girl and finally lose his virginity.

- *Little Miss Sunshine:* Everyone in the family momentarily gives up whatever is preoccupying them individually. They give up their self-involvement and their focus on their own problems as they come together for Olive.

- *Thelma & Louise:* They ultimately give up their lives for freedom.

- *The King's Speech:* Bertie gives up his terror of the opposition and his haughtiness and pretense of invulnerability and thus grows stronger and more self-aware. He finally is able to speak with dignity.

- *Roman Holiday*: The princess makes the hard choice to give up a chance at love with Joe Bradley and to continue in her role with the monarchy, but now it's going to be on her terms. She gets something she needed: a greater sense of self. Joe gives up the opportunity to print the story and thereby win the bet with his editor, but he gains her respect and heartfelt affection, even if he doesn't walk away with the girl.

OTHER THINGS THAT OFTEN HAPPEN IN ACT III:

- Epiphanies: Generally these happen toward the end of Act II or in Act III as the hero effectively sees the light. Michael admits to Julie: "I was a better man as a woman with you than I ever was with a woman as a man." Thelma says, "I feel awake." Buzz recognizes that to be a toy is a great thing. Andy is able to recognize that all along he was waiting for Trish. The princess is no longer taking orders or going to be straitjacketed by her royal position.

- A bringing together of all the characters: All the characters are often reunited, especially in lighter genre stories with happy endings. *The 40-Year-Old Virgin* and *Toy Story* are good examples.

Finally, endings are tough. I always seem to struggle with them, which is all the more reason why you should do as I say, even if I don't always do, when it comes to figuring out where you want to wind up before you set out on your journey.

And when in doubt, assuming you're not writing a tragedy, I would say err on the side of William Goldman's advice, "People want to believe nice things." You don't have to tie everything up neatly with a bow; in fact, it's often better if you don't. But it's my opinion that you want at least to leave people with a glimmer of hope. *Sideways, Little Miss Sunshine, Thelma & Louise, Roman Holiday*—none of these films show their hero(es) getting exactly what they thought they wanted. But they either get the hope of attaining it or perhaps something even better: a freer, fuller, more authentic life.

ACT III TAKEAWAYS:

1. Act III is about "do or die," literally or figuratively. It's where the hero faces his biggest test of all.

2. Act III is about stakes, and these ought to significant. It's about the "or else...." If your hero doesn't achieve his goal, what's the worst that can happen to him? What's the alternative that he cannot abide?

3. Act III is also about the completion of the character arc. It's where that transformation, assuming there is one, is made clear. It's about demonstrating how your hero has grown, changed and evolved.

4. Act III answers the main question posed in Act I.

5. Ideally, you want your story and its intensity to build as you approach the end.

ACT III WORKSHEET:

1. Does your hero take some sort of positive action at the beginning of Act III in order to spring back from the low Plot Point #2?

2. Is there a battle won at the end of Act II/ beginning of Act III, but is the war not yet over?

3. Does your Act III answer the question raised by Plot Point #1 in Act I?

4. Does your hero ultimately achieve what he went after in the

first place (his goal)? Does he gain something else, either in addition or instead?

5. Does he get what he needed in emotional growth terms? Is he different at the end of the story from the person he was when it began?

6. How, specifically, is this transformation demonstrated?

7. Is the urgency of your story intensifying as you approach the end?

8. Is your hero actively driving the story by this point?

9. By the end, has your hero claimed (or reclaimed) his power? Is he living more fully?

10. What do you imagine is your final image?

11. What feeling do you want the audience to leave the theater with after seeing your movie?

12. Have you created an Act III Beat Sheet so that you now have an overview and roadmap of your entire story?

STRUCTURALLY SPEAKING: ARGO

READ: ARGO Screenplay
(http://screenplayexplorer.com/wp-content/scripts/argo.pdf)

Screenplay by: Chris Terrio

Based on: *The Master of Disguise* by Antonio J. Mendez and the *Wired Magazine* article "The Great Escape" by Joshuah Bearman

For my money, *Argo* is a very good movie. It's not a perfect one—how many are?—but it has an awful lot going for it, first and foremost its fascinating stranger-than-fiction true premise. At its core is the delicious and absurd idea that a schlocky, pretend Hollywood movie turns out to be the solution to one of the more vexing international political problems of the day.

It's a smart script, masterfully directed and edited. There's effective use of actual footage intercut with dramatic re-creation, multiple points of view, and wonderful attention to period and visual detail. The chaos in the streets—a car ablaze, a corpse hanging from a lamppost—co-exists with life going on as usual, traffic jams and people lunching in sidewalk cafes, creating a steady sense of foreboding, underlying tension. (Note that these details are not simply directorial choices but things that are on the page. See for yourself when you read the script.)

The interesting and enlivening shift in tone once the Hollywood plan is hatched provides a fun, comic element. Also, the script has a solid structure and a steadily building story, if not a particularly convincing character arc (in my humble opinion its one shortcoming). But talk about a movie in which everything is leading to the ending!

ACT I
It starts off with a quick bit of voice-over exposition filling us in on

the events that preceded the Iranian hostage crisis. Interesting visuals, news footage, storyboards, and illustrations set the scene, which then shifts into real time with a bang. The re-creation of the storming of the U.S. embassy in Tehran and the desperate attempts by those inside to destroy material and escape the invaders is brilliantly staged, fast-paced, and genuinely terrifying.

From a purely character-establishing standpoint, however, this opening is slightly tricky in that there are a multitude of players to follow and no time to learn even what their names are, let alone distinguish who is who or what makes any of them tick. Regardless, we feel for them, as they're people under attack, and the sequence is gripping. The opening twelve minutes basically function as prologue; there is no main character, only a set-up of the situation/crisis.

The hero, Tony Mendez, played by Ben Affleck, is introduced relatively late, (13 minutes in), and structurally it's a just a little tricky in that the problem he is given to remedy is not intrinsically his own. He's not a hostage, so it's not his personal predicament that he's trying to overcome/solve. He's not even someone who is related to any of the diplomats who are attacked or even someone whose job/livelihood appears to depend on his freeing them.

Inciting Incident: We meet Mendez when he receives the phone call telling him of the takeover of the American embassy. Shortly thereafter we're filled in more via a conversation between him and his boss, played by Bryan Cranston, though it's still a bit unclear what anyone's actual job is. Exposition is ladled out as necessary. We learn Mendez is an "exfil" guy. (That's short for exfiltration, as in the opposite of infiltration. Who knew?) Anyway, here we also get a bit more information about the six Americans who are now hiding in the Canadian ambassador's home, via a slide show.

The connection between who Tony is as a human being, how he personally might need to grow or change, and how the task he's assigned might catalyze that change is tenuous at best. The scenes that establish his home life, or more accurately a lack thereof, feel a little perfunctory and a bit shoe-horned in. He feels slightly like a blank slate, but perhaps this was intentional, as he is, after all, a spy. From a certain angle, maybe we're not supposed to feel like we really know him?

I say this not to nitpick the film, which I like a lot, but to point out that it's extremely hard to do everything "right." There are so many balls to juggle when writing a script that if you manage to genuinely excel in even a few areas, you'll be ahead of the game and be cut some slack in others. I think the lack of connection we make with Mendez and who he really is as a human being, and how that vagueness contributes to a less convincing character arc is the one weak point of the film. But as the rest of the story is so dramatically compelling and engaging, this small shortcoming winds up ultimately mattering relatively little.

Anyway, at this point it becomes clear that Mendez is essentially the main character as he is charged with figuring out how to get the Americans out. He's the guy with a mission.

At 23 minutes in, after other escape plans are suggested and shot down, Mendez suggests his outlandish-sounding solution, "the best bad idea" they have: They'll pretend that the six are a Canadian film crew looking for a location for a sci-fi movie. Mendez, posing as a producer, will fly in and accompany them as they fly out together.

Plot Point #1:
Mendez's plan is approved, the Feds agree to send him to L.A. to put the scheme in motion. This action spins the story in a new direction not only dramatically and geographically but also tonally, from the deadly serious to the suddenly more comic and fun.

ACT II

Change of scenery to L.A. Lots of funny clever jokes and comic relief at the expense of the b.s. of the film business courtesy of John Goodman as a makeup artist who, we're told, does occasional prosthetic work for the CIA, and Alan Arkin, in a brilliant Oscar-nominated performance as the seasoned, slightly washed-up producer Lester Siegel. These two, whose help Mendez enlists, are arguably two of the most interesting characters in the film.

After all the historical re-creation and drama, now it feels like the movie really takes off and hits its stride. This is the fun and games section of the film, where things take this very unexpected turn. Certainly this almost absurdist aspect of the story is one of the main elements one assumes inspired the people involved to want to make the movie in the first place.

Meanwhile, the tension in Washington and Tehran continues to be ratcheted up with the news that the Iranian guard at the airport has been increased. And the Hollywood sequence is repeatedly cross-cut with actual news footage, reenactments, and scenes of tensions rising in both DC and at the ambassador's residence in Tehran to great effect.

Midpoint: Mendez is given the green light. He heads to Iran.

The film morphs a bit again here, this time into a bona fide spy thriller, and the suspense really starts to build. The six Americans hiding out are given the roles they're to play, and there's a particularly nerve-wracking sequence as they're forced to make their way through the local bazaar in an attempt to prove they really are a film crew on a location scout.

Plot Point #2:

This occurs at 77 minutes into a 120-minute film, so just slightly early by conventional standards. This is obviously to allow for an extended third act and the movie's main *raison d'etre*, the escape from Tehran.

The all-is-lost moment occurs when Tony's boss (Cranston) calls him at the last minute to tell him the mission has been called off. (Interestingly, according to an online review of the film, the actual mission was not almost called off at the last minute and Mendez didn't go against orders to try to bring the six back. Nor was there any scary interrogation at the airport or the last-minute uncertainty in terms of whether or not the escapees would get on the plane but, dramatically speaking, the movie-makers needed a Plot Point #2. This is what you call artistic license, and it definitely does make for a more powerful, more suspenseful story.)

Regardless, here Mendez is told the Joint Chiefs are planning a rescue of the hostages and they fear Mendez's plan could be exposed. The connection between these two things—and why one might preclude the other—was just slightly murky to me, but the point is that Mendez is ordered to abandon the mission.

Here, we as the audience have what is called "superior position." We know something most of the characters don't: that their fate in Iran has been sealed, they're not going to get out after all. This creates a lot of dramatic tension, especially as we watch Mendez decide to keep that bad news from them and see how it haunts him.

ACT III

Note that overall, the story is building throughout, particularly here in Act III, where the tension and pace accelerate. The plot is not wandering. It's crystal-clear who the hero is, what his goal is, what the stakes are, and who the opposition is.

Mendez bounces back from Plot Point 2, deciding to buck authority and go through with his plan anyway. Come hell or high water, he's going to do his best to get these people out, and this all makes for powerful nail-biting, edge-of-your-seat stuff.

Also, he faces his biggest test(s) of all here in order to achieve his global goal: He has to run the gauntlet of getting them to the airport; through security, where they all have to convincingly play their parts; through an extended interrogation scene; and finally onto the plane. The tension is maintained even once they're all seated on the plane, with the final chase on the tarmac and an overwhelming sense of catharsis when the plane finally takes flight.

When the moment finally arrives that the passengers are told they're out of Iranian air space, the elation is palpable. Yet it takes a long time for anyone on the plane to get around to thanking Tony, and when one guy finally does, it's restrained. This was clearly a conscious creative choice on the part of the filmmakers. I guess the point was that Mendez was a bit of an enigma, emotionally cool and even closed off, and thus that made him good at his job, if not quite as appealing as a hero.

Finally, the coda of Mendez's reunion with his estranged wife and child felt a bit tacked on and contrived to me. I get that we're to believe that he is, by virtue of this experience, somehow a changed man. Perhaps if time had been spent in the beginning illustrating how he'd taken his family for granted, or had been a less-than-attentive father and husband, this bit might be more moving. Although that is implied by his separation, we're not given many real details or reason to *feel* it. But I can also completely understand why no screen time was devoted to this, as it's not what the movie is really about. Still, it might've been nice to feel a bit more for him personally at the very end.

CHAPTER NINE

BUILDING CHARACTER(S) PART ONE: HEROES

> "Character cannot be developed in ease and quiet. Only through the experience of trial and suffering can the soul be strengthened, ambition inspired and success achieved."
>
> ~ Helen Keller

I'VE GONE OVER THE PURPOSE of stories and the general framework for laying one out, but obviously the key element in any story is the "who." The people (and sometimes other creatures) who inhabit stories are what we relate to and care about. Most truly memorable movies are about memorable characters. In terms of franchises, Indiana Jones, Jason Bourne, Katniss Everdeen, Tony Stark, Shrek, Captain Jack Sparrow, and James Bond are some of the distinctive individuals around whom successful series are built. It's the characters we go to see again and again in new adventures.

But creating a fully dimensional hero whom an audience will find compelling and relate to can be challenging. As a result, a note screenwriters often get is that they need to make their hero more sympathetic, more likable. Reasonable enough in theory, but how exactly? It's a little vague, like telling a chef to make a meal taste better. But, as with cooking, if you break it down, I believe there are some time-tested techniques that can help lead an audience to care about what happens to your hero.

FIVE TIPS FOR MAKING US CARE ABOUT YOUR HERO:

1. MAKE HIM "NICE"

As in real life, we tend to like the person who is kind to children, old people, and small animals. The witty, generous, principled, clever, resourceful, helpful, polite, thoughtful, self-deprecating person is "likable." This is not rocket science; it's something we all understand on a very basic level. Thus, one technique that's often employed to get audiences to relate to and root for a hero is the small, kind gesture, typically exhibited toward one less powerful, that tells us someone is good.

Blake Snyder's screenwriting book, *Save the Cat*, is named for precisely this approach of having your hero make some small, sometimes very small, kind gesture early in the film that shows us he's got a good heart.

I find this sort of tactic a bit obvious and creaky, but if you can find a way to put a fresh spin on it, to make it feel genuinely organic to the story and not just shoe-horned in, it can be useful. That said, although nice behavior can make us like someone, at least in a superficial way, it can also feel generic and bland. For that reason, you're also going to want to:

2. TORMENT HIM

As the writer/creator, generally you want to fall in love with your hero; you want to understand him and to see him succeed at achieving whatever he's after. And then you must torture him mercilessly on the road to it.

What really takes things up another notch in terms of making us want to root for a hero is to have him be *treated unfairly by the fates*.

I believe that most of us have an intrinsic sense of justice, especially when we're objective observers, when we have no dog of our own in the fight. We all want to believe there is a somehow a fundamental fairness at work in the world, and yet we all also know that life simply isn't fair. Still, we relate to and feel for someone who we feel has suffered an injustice, at the hands of another person, or an institution, or simply cruel fate. Thus, the person who is disabled, an orphan, discriminated against, stricken by disease, stolen from, jilted, bereaved, falsely accused, abused, ridiculed, or just plain unlucky and struggling to get along in this life is almost automatically inherently sympathetic.

Taking this thinking a step further, what we are *most* sympathetic to, what tugs at our heartstrings even more firmly, is someone who has been treated unfairly by the fates but who, instead of lying down and feeling sorry for himself, decides to stand up and fight. That fight, that willingness to determinedly go after whatever it is he most wants and not give up, is what engages our sympathies most of all.

This is what we root for and, not incidentally, what we aspire to be able to do in our own lives when the going gets tough and world beats us down. We all know only too well that we can't control everything that happens to us, but to the extent that we can control how we respond, *that* is what truly matters; that is what defines us.

> "Be kind, for everyone you ever meet is fighting a hard battle."
>
> ~ Ian Maclaren

Take a look at a few Oscar-winning screenplays and see how many deal with a hero who's been somehow unfairly treated by the fates and who then has to transcend himself in order to live a freer, fuller life: *Good Will Hunting, Erin Brockovich, Moonstruck, Rocky, The King's Speech, Forrest Gump, Precious, Slumdog Millionaire, Little Miss Sunshine, Silver Linings Playbook, Shine*— the list goes on and on.

Further Examples of a Bad Hand:

- *The 40-Year-Old Virgin*: Andy, a shy, sweet, genuinely nice guy, has been unlucky in love (and sex) and as a result has pretty much given up on it.

- *Argo*: This film represents a slight variation on this principle in that Tony Mendez, the hero, doesn't seem to have been treated particularly unfairly by the fates and, perhaps consequently, doesn't seem to have a very convincing character arc, and what there is of one regarding his personal life feels a bit contrived. But the characters whom he sets out to help have definitely been dealt a massive blow; they're people faithfully doing their jobs in Tehran when suddenly their world is upended and they become hunted and effectively imprisoned.

- *Little Miss Sunshine*: Talk about treated unfairly by the fates! As the story opens, the matriarch of the family, Sheryl, is at the hospital picking up her brother, who has just tried to commit suicide over a failed love affair. Her husband is a delusional wanna-be self-help guru who has yet to turn a profit at it and thus is basically unemployed. His elderly father is a drug addict who's been kicked out of his assisted living facility. Her teenage son is angry and sullen and recently has become intentionally mute. Interestingly, the least troubled of all the characters is the little girl, Olive, around whom the story— and family—revolves.

- *Thelma & Louise*: Thelma is attacked and almost raped by a creep she'd just met a country western bar.

- *The King's Speech*: The Duke of York, Bertie, was abused as a child, has a speech impediment, and has been bullied and underestimated as a result.

- *Sideways*: Miles is a genuinely talented and dedicated writer, one who has worked very hard at his craft, but despite his sincere and worthy efforts, he is told there is no room in the marketplace for his work.

- *Good Will Hunting*: Matt Damon's Will was physically and emotionally abused as a child. Sean, his therapist, played by Robin Williams, has lost his wife to cancer.

So ask yourself: How has your hero been dealt an unfair blow or suffered some sort of injustice? Put simply, how has he been hurt? It can be part of the backstory, as in *Bridesmaids*, where we learn Annie lost her dream of owning a bakery to a lousy economy; or as in *The King's Speech* or *Good Will Hunting*, where we learn that the leads had been abused as children.

Or the blow can happen after the story begins as, for example, in *Finding Nemo*, when little clownfish Nemo's mother and all his would-be siblings are killed in the rather shockingly dark opening sequence and shortly thereafter he's abducted by a diver. Another example where the blow comes shortly after the story begins is *Gone With the Wind*, which starts in the last privileged moments of Scarlett O'Hara's life, which is soon turned upside down by the Civil War.

Once you've considered what wound your hero may have suffered, you'll want to be sure to:

3. IDENTIFY WHAT HE WANTS

This may seem obvious, but you'd be surprised how many scripts I read in which the thing the hero is after is unclear. What he wants is his goal, and the action he takes in pursuit of that goal is the engine of your story. The goal can be anything, but it needs to be clear and specific, certainly by the end of the first act. Equally important, the audience ought to be able to understand why the hero wants this particular thing so much; to understand what larger significance it has for him. The complications that result and obstacles that arise will then test your hero's mettle and force him to prove how badly he wants to achieve it.

Once you've identified his goal, then you'll also want to:

4. IDENTIFY (for yourself) WHAT HE NEEDS

You want to think about how he needs to change or grow in order to live a fuller, freer life. Even if you never have the character say this outright (and you probably shouldn't), you'll want to know.

This, if you work backward, means that at the beginning of the story you have to determine in what way(s) your hero has been complicit in his own misery, how he has not been living his best life thus far.

Has he been resigned, selling himself short or settling because he didn't have the courage to fight for something better? Was he complacent? Lazy? Naive? Too timid? Too cynical? Too self-centered? Whatever it is, this quality is what will underlie his character arc. It points to what he needs to learn, the way in which he needs to grow in character over the course of the story.

Wants and Needs Examples:

- In *Toy Story*, what Woody wants is to get rid of Buzz. What he needs is to learn some humility, to learn how to share and be a team player.

- In *The 40-Year-Old Virgin*, what Andy wants is to lose his virginity. What he needs is to grow up and learn how to engage in an honest, intimate, adult relationship.

- In *Little Miss Sunshine*, what the family ostensibly wants is for Olive to win the beauty pageant. What they need is to learn to how come together and support one another.

- In *The King's Speech*, what Bertie wants is simply to learn how to speak without stuttering. What he needs, in order to achieve this goal, is to confront and make peace with the emotional wounds of his childhood.

- In *Good Will Hunting*, what Matt Damon's character Will wants is to get paroled after a number of run-ins with the law. He makes a deal to go into therapy in order to achieve that but initially is a reluctant participant. What he needs, and what his relationship with his therapist ultimately enables him to achieve, is to heal enough and learn to trust enough to be able to open his heart to other people.

Finally, you're going to want to:

5. MAKE HIM *REALLY* FIGHT FOR IT

Your hero has been mistreated, cheated, abused, abandoned, betrayed, taken advantage of, injured, or just plain unlucky, and perhaps thus far in life has settled for this status quo. Or maybe his status quo is actually pretty great to begin with and perhaps he's a little smug. Either way, something happens, that unexpected bolt from the blue strikes, upending his status quo and typically ratcheting up the pressure on him.

Now he has a problem and, as previously mentioned, *the movie is what he DOES about it.* It's the action he takes to try to change his situation, how he fights to overcome whatever obstacles he encounters on the road to the goal he's identified for himself and how he grows as a human being over the course of that journey. Remember, you want your "lead" to *lead,* to be as proactive as possible, not just reactive, especially as your story progresses.

In the case of each of the films mentioned above, the hero is struggling as the story opens and must take some sort of action, and that requires courage and usually very hard work. His ability to summon this courage and face whatever obstacles may come is at the heart of what makes us invest.

Movies are about that point in a character's life when he is forced to rise to the occasion. And the more unfairly the fates and/or the villain(s) have conspired against him, the more unjustly he's been treated and the harder he fights to overcome whatever obstacles are thrown in his path en route to his goal, the more invested we become in his struggle.

OBSTACLES are the universe's way of saying to your hero, "Just how badly do you want it?" And his answer ought to be "Very badly."

You must make your hero *prove* how much he wants whatever it is that he wants. What must he give up, learn, endure in order to get it? How must he grow and fight in order to achieve his goal? What courage must he summon or develop? If you work backward in terms of his character arc, this means you have to give him somewhere to go, someplace to start from so that he has room to grow over the course of the story.

Not only do you want to throw plenty of obstacles in his path, it's important to set him up in the beginning in such a way that he has somehow *been complicit in his own troubles*. Because we all can change only ourselves, right? In the end, the only things over which any of us have any real control are ourselves and our response to any particular situation. Although characters are not responsible for what was done to them, they are responsible for how they respond, and therein their true power lies.

In *Bridesmaids*, we learn early on the backstory that Kristen Wiig's Annie had thrown her heart and soul and all her money into opening a bakery, which failed. She had tried her best but lost pretty much everything. In this, she's immediately sympathetic; she's talented and had worked hard and by rights didn't deserve her bad fortune, but the larger economic collapse fell on her as it did on everyone. Since then, she's become passive, somewhat paralyzed and caught up in feeling sorry for herself. Her flaw is that she has given up and wallowed too long in self-pity.

As Megan (Melissa McCarthy's character) ultimately tells her, "You're your problem, and you're your solution." What your hero learns, how he changes as a result of taking the journey of the story, is what enables him to somehow live a better, freer, more authentic and productive life by the end.

It's my contention that the reason stories like this have so much resonance for audiences is because almost everyone on some level sees himself as an underdog. Everyone, no matter how seemingly powerful, has his own battles to fight. Rare to downright nonexistent is the person who hasn't at one time or another felt lonely, afraid, anxious, vulnerable, hurt, betrayed, underestimated, etc. We're all mortal, flesh and blood, and we all suffer our own particular slings and arrows.

Thus the underdog is a particularly powerful, relatable and universal archetype. In fact, if you want to play the odds, I would suggest you write an underdog story. *Slumdog Millionaire, Erin Brockovich, Rocky, Cinderella, Bridesmaids*—there are a million of them. The archetype is tried and true and will work again and again. And if movies are about the moment when somebody's life changed, then some of the most satisfying movies are about this transformation—about seeing the unlikely one, the underdog, succeed. And the bigger the underdog someone is, the more unlikely he is to triumph, typically the bigger the character arc and the more audiences tend to eat it up.

Almost everybody loves a story about a person whose potential and gifts have gone unappreciated, if not been squandered, who then summons his courage and somehow fights for and gets his shot, and who comes into full possession of his power and thereby improves his lot in life. These difficult experiences, in their infinite variety yet universal commonality, are part of the human condition, so we feel for characters who find themselves in challenging situations, particularly when they're not primarily of their own making.

When someone has been unjustly victimized, underestimated by the world, treated unfairly, etc. and then, rather than roll over and die, decides to take a stand and really fight for a better life, that makes us want to root for him more than almost anything else. That fight, the digging deep and summoning of the courage and willingness to face down one's fears and demons, both internal and external—to do whatever it takes and not give up—is at the heart of what makes us invest and care.

> *What defines us is how well we rise after falling.*

So before you start down the road of writing your script, see if you can pin down these signposts which can help keep you on track: Think about your hero's wound, identify both what he wants and what he needs, and then really force him to struggle, fight and ultimately change somehow in order to achieve his goal. Keeping these elements in mind will help you to create both a hero your audience will relate to emotionally and a story they'll find compelling.

BUCKING THE CHARACTER ARC PARADIGM

There has been something of a mini-trend lately on the part of writers to eschew the traditional character arc. Because of the dogma of so many screenwriting books and gurus regarding it, and the seeming obligation to make a main character somehow change and grow over the course of the story, there's bound to be a backlash.

Moneyball and *Young Adult* are two examples of fairly recent films in which the "heroes" don't really change or improve much by the end of the movie. But I would argue that in both of these cases, something else does: the outer world's perception of them.

Regardless, I can certainly understand, having been tethered for so long to the idea that the hero must somehow become a better person by the end of the story, why some writers choose to go in the opposite direction. (The writers of *Seinfeld* famously had a guiding mantra of "no hugging, no learning." But then that's TV and not feature film). Anyway, the idea that the hero must grow and become "better" can admittedly sometimes feel mechanical or contrived when characters seem to suddenly change not so much because it's organic to the story and narratively logical or justified, but because it's understood to be commercially required.

But although writers should absolutely feel free to make whatever creative choices they deem appropriate for the story they're telling, I would argue that, generally speaking, movies in which the protagonist does not grow by the end are usually inherently less satisfying for an audience and thus often less commercially successful. They simply don't usually resonate as much for most of us or feed us in the same way that stories in which the hero somehow learns or improves do. I'm not saying don't do this, but if you do, you want to be intentional about it, and you should know going in that you're setting yourself a higher bar, not only in terms of getting your work sold but also in terms of making people care about and relate to your hero and his story.

WRITING FOR STARS

With the changes in the movie business in the last ten to fifteen years—with the franchise or brand becoming such a dominant force—star-power, the ability of a particular actor or actress to get an original movie made or draw a massive audience, has admittedly been somewhat diminished.

Still, if your goal is to try to sell a spec screenplay (meaning one that is not part of an already established franchise), particularly a script that will be substantially expensive to produce, one of your best bets remains to try to interest "elements," i.e., stars and/or a name director. To do this, you'll want to create roles stars will want to play.

Stars want to flex their muscles, so really put them through their paces. Give your hero something genuinely formidable to overcome and the ability and traits to do it. His character can be flawed—in fact, it probably should be flawed in order to give him room to grow—but don't forget to also give him his virtues. Let him be clever, bold, brave, charming, resourceful, endearing, graceful (or better yet witty) under pressure, strong, decent, smart, powerful, perceptive, courageous, sincere, insightful, lovable, principled, sympathetic. And if not all the way through, then certainly give him a virtue or two by the end.

HERO CHARACTER DEVELOPMENT TAKEAWAYS:

1. You want to torment your hero on the road to his goal. Don't make things too easy on him. This *builds character*.

2. What your hero does to try to solve his problem—the *action* he takes to achieve his goal and the complications that result—is the engine of the movie.

3. Your hero should be complicit in his own troubles. That is, when the story begins, he should in some way, possibly a variety of ways, not be living his best life, as this is what gives him room to grow.

4. How the hero changes as a person over the course of the story is his character arc.

5. Audiences generally like a positive character arc, even if they're not consciously aware of it. Eliminate or subvert it at your own risk.

HERO CHARACTER DEVELOPMENT WORKSHEET:

1. What does your hero want? What is his identified, specific external goal? Can an audience understand why he wants this so much?

2. What does he need? In emotional terms, how might he need to change or grow as a human being?

3. Has he somehow been treated unfairly by the fates? Has he suffered some sort of wound, either in backstory or after the story begins?

4. Has he been complicit in his circumstances because of some character flaw? (This complicity or flaw ought to be established in Act I and is connected to both his external goal and to his character arc.)

5. What specific behavior of his tells us this?

6. Why should/would an audience care about what happens to him and want to root for him? How is he sympathetic?

STRUCTURALLY SPEAKING: IRON MAN

Screenplay by: Mark Fergus, Hawk Ostby, Art Marcum, Matt Holloway

Based on Characters by: Stan Lee, Don Heck, Larry Lieber, Jack Kirby

Unfortunately, this script is not available online. There are transcripts, but these are not particularly useful for our purposes. If anyone can find a copy, please drop me an email at diane@dianedrake.com and I'll add a link here.

ACT I

As you know, typically the first thing that happens in a movie is the establishment of the status quo. Action movies, however, are often a bit of an exception to this principle in that their makers seem to feel obliged to open with a bang. You see this a lot in the Bond movies and many others, particularly action franchises.

I assume the filmmakers figure that people have paid their $12 and bought their popcorn and when they sit down in the theater, they expect some action, pronto. So the studios deliver. Movies in this genre often start off with an immediate high-adrenaline sequence, then backtrack or slow down, comparatively speaking, to set up the status quo and story. *Iron Man* is a perfect example of this technique.

We open on cocky wise guy Tony Stark visiting Afghanistan for a live demonstration of his company's latest weapons system, the Jericho missile. Things quickly go awry, however, when the convoy he's riding in is attacked by local warlords and he is taken prisoner.

Cut to: "36 hours earlier," where a voiceover at an awards

banquet gives us the exposition and backstory regarding this wunderkind: Tony Stark is a genius, weapons-inventor, billionaire, playboy. We also see where and how he lives like a rock star, and meet his business partner Obadiah Stane (there's an evil-sounding villain's name for you), played by Jeff Bridges, and Stark's long-suffering assistant, who's also a little in love with him, Pepper Potts (Gwyneth Paltrow).

Soon, Stark is on the plane to Afghanistan for his company's military dog and pony show, accompanied by a colonel played by Terrence Howard, his main G man. The status quo is established just in time for the opening sequence to be revisited; now the attack functions as the **Inciting Incident** (bolt from the blue/cause for all that follows) at 16 minutes in. We're now back to the point where his convoy is blown up and he's taken hostage, and from here the story moves forward.

With the aid of a fellow prisoner doctor, who has implanted a sort of jerry-rigged magnet in Tony's chest ostensibly to keep shrapnel from entering his heart, Stark is nursed back to health. His captors allow this because they want him to build them their own missile. At first he refuses then relents when he comes up with a plan to instead fabricate a suit of iron that will allow him to escape.

Plot Point #1 (38 minutes in).
He painstakingly builds the suit, but just as he's almost finished, the bad guys catch on. Another major action sequence follows as he dons the suit, battles to escape, bids farewell to the dying doctor, and finally takes flight out of there.

ACT II

Stark manages to make it back to the US and his mad genius laboratory, where he sets about inventing the ultimate high-tech version of the suit. This portion of the script lives up to its fun and games reputation as Stark goes through lots of comedic trial and error, bickers with his robotic assistants and flirts with his human one, Miss Potts, in the process.

Meantime, he's growing as a character. He has an epiphany about his work and its effect in the world and announces at a press conference that he no longer wants to be in the weapons business. This news doesn't sit especially well with his business partner or the board of his company, but he's not particularly worried; the work is now what matters most to him.

Midpoint: After much effort, the new high-tech suit is finally complete and it works! He takes flight in it, this time into the stratosphere. (1 hour, 2 minutes into a 2-hour, 7 minute movie).

But after this flight and his subsequent further flirtation and dancing with Pepper at a charity gathering (the other part of his character arc being that he's evidently grown tired of the bimbos and has started to truly appreciate Pepper and see her in a new light), the fun and games section of the story winds down. Now, in the second half of Act II, the threats, both at home and abroad, escalate.

At the charity event, he's confronted with photos of the slaughter of innocent civilians using weapons with his name on them. Suspecting that his business partners have been selling to both sides, Stark confronts Obadiah, who in essence admits that it's true and that he was the one who led the effort to force Tony out of the company.

Shortly thereafter, Tony, as Iron Man, takes off for that distant village where the warlords are threatening the innocent. He efficiently dispatches the bad guys, rescues the captives, withstands a missile attack, and even outmaneuvers and survives a run-in with his own military when they mistake him for an enemy. There are plenty of ups and downs, twist and turns, both literal and figurative, in this sequence. Thus, he convincingly demonstrates how truly badass Iron Man is.

But unfortunately for Tony, it now appears that his two worst enemies—the warlord who originally took him prisoner and Obadiah—are in cahoots. The brutal Afghan shares with Obadiah the details about the metal suit Tony created while there, and now Obadiah has a blueprint to create one of his own.

Suspicious of Obadiah, Tony enlists a reluctant Pepper to break into the company computer system and see what he's been up to. There's a suspenseful, tension-filled sequence as she does so and discovers that he's been trying to do Tony in, when suddenly Obadiah himself shows up. He knows.

Plot Point #2:

Shortly thereafter, Obadiah appears in Tony's pad and subjects him to the same paralysis-generating gadget we'd previously seen him use on the warlord. A frozen Tony is forced to listen and watch mutely as, in classic comic book villain fashion, Obadiah removes Tony's heart-protecting generator—the key to powering the suit—and spells out the details of his evil plan, which includes killing Pepper. Then he disappears, leaving a devastated, still-paralyzed Tony all alone, (1 hour, 39 minutes in, leaving 28 minutes for Act III).

ACT III

Tony refuses to roll over and die. He struggles to get to the old model heart-saving gadget which he'd previously told Pepper to destroy, but which she'd instead turned into a paperweight as a gift for him.

Meanwhile, Obadiah powers up his own Iron Man suit, and now it's on. Obadiah comes thundering after Pepper, and Tony, back in the game with the aid of the colonel, soon comes flying in to her defense. What follows is a massive battle of the titans across the city, where, of course, our hero seems vastly outmatched by the ginormous Goliath Obadiah. But Tony is smarter and, with Pepper's help, he manages to blow up the reactor at Stark headquarters, thus vanquishing his nemesis and yet, of course, miraculously surviving himself.

If the third act of this film feels a little contrived and perfunctory (as it does to me anyway), the final scene redeems it. The last sequence in the film finds the colonel giving another press conference regarding the recent events at Stark headquarters while Pepper and Tony flirt and spar backstage. Before Tony goes on stage, he's given his alibi talking points so as to throw the public off the scent of Iron Man's true identity. Thus, the misdirection and surprise of his final line, where he blurts out, "I *am* Iron Man," was so great it made me laugh out loud, and yet it was also completely in keeping with his character.

Other fun facts: Writer/director Jon Favreau has a cameo as Iron Man's bodyguard; the creator of Iron Man, Stan Lee, said the character was inspired by Howard Hughes.

CHAPTER TEN

BUILDING CHARACTER(S) PART TWO: VILLAINS, CO- STARS AND EVERYBODY ELSE

> *"Kites rise highest against the wind."*
>
> ~ Winston Churchill

I'VE TALKED A GREAT DEAL about he hero and his mission, but of course the vast majority of movies aren't about just one main character. The hero has to have other characters to fight against or to align with, and incidental players who serve a variety of other story purposes. In a well-structured film, there are usually several supporting players, sometimes co-stars/buddies, and often a main ANTAGONIST or VILLAIN for the hero to face off against.

Naturally, a villain character isn't suited to all stories, but a great villain in the right context can really help keep your script compelling, keep the tension high, keep the conflict clear and keep viewers engaged. And the stronger the villain, the more evil, clever and seemingly all-powerful he is, the stronger your hero must become in order to defeat him. The hero must rise to meet him.

> *"Love your enemies, because they are instruments to your destiny."*
>
> ~ Joseph Campbell, myth expert and author *The Hero of a Thousand Faces* (upon which filmmaker George Lucas drew heavily for the *Star Wars* movies)

Hard as Campbell's advice above may sometimes be to put into practice in real life, I think this is another of the overall lessons of story. Your villain, in fact every obstacle you throw in your hero's path over the course of the story, *is* an instrument of his destiny. In a structural sense, the villain is there to bring—to force—the hero to a higher realization of himself.

I recently read a classic book from the 1970s called *The Inner Game of Tennis*, by W. Timothy Gallwey. He had this to say regarding the value of competition in sports:

> *"The surfer waits for the big wave because he values the challenge it presents. He values the obstacles the wave puts between him and his goal of riding the wave to the beach. Why? Because it is those very obstacles, the size and churning power of the wave, which draw from the surfer his greatest effort. It is only against the big waves that he is required to use all his skill, all his courage and concentration to overcome; only then can he realize the true limits of his capacities. At that point he often attains his peak.*
>
> *In other words, the more challenging the obstacle he faces, the greater the opportunity for the surfer to discover and extend his true potential.* **The potential may have always been within him, but until it is manifested in action, it remains a secret hidden from himself. The obstacles are a very necessary ingredient to this process of self-discovery."*

His description of the purpose of the wave is perfectly analogous to the purpose of the villain and to the purpose of challenges and obstacles in general. Seen from this perspective, they are there to bring people to the highest manifestation of themselves.

When it comes to drawing villains, though, remember we're really not looking to understand them. In fact, our lack of knowledge about the villain's backstory and what made him who and what he is—what unfair blows the universe may have sent *his* way—is actually integral to our seeing him as the villain; otherwise we might sympathize with him. But it's not his story, it's our hero's story, and it's our hero's job to vanquish him.

In his TED talk, filmmaker Andrew Stanton shared a quote from the kids' television host Mr. Rogers which he said Rogers carried in his wallet: "There isn't anyone you couldn't learn to love once you've heard their story." The inverse of this is largely true in the case of antagonists, we generally don't know their stories.

But even if we don't know, and don't need to know, the specific reasons why a villain is so "villainous", I have a theory about evil: Insecurity is the root of it. Scratch an angry, hateful person and you'll find a frightened one inside. Whether you agree with my assumption or not, you might ask yourself, what is my villain insecure about? What is he overcompensating for? What is he afraid of? How does the hero press his buttons and vice versa? How does the hero threaten him?

For my money, the best villains often don't initially necessarily seem like villains. They seem fair-minded, even likable, until you realize that they use their calm reasonableness to disguise their nefarious motives. True sociopaths who don't overtly look or act like villains, who are able to cloak their deeper evil with a superficial amiability and even charm, are to me far more chilling than the over-the-top Freddie Kruger sort.

Nurse Ratched in *One Flew Over the Cuckoo's Nest*, Little Bill Daggett in *Unforgiven*, the computer Hal in *2001: A Space Odyssey*, Paul Reiser in *Aliens*—these to me are some genuinely terrifying villains who, on the surface, initially appear to be the epitome of calm rationality. One of the most frightening moments I can recall ever watching in a theater is also one of the quietest. In fact, it's silent. It's the moment in *Aliens* when Paul Reiser simply casually switches off the monitor that shows Sigourney Weaver is trapped in a room with an alien, believing he's sealed her death.

But evil comes in all variations. Sid, the vicious neighbor kid in *Toy Story,* is another example of a great villain and he's obviously not a subtle one. I find Sid fascinating in that the creators of *Toy Story* opted to really go dark with him. Sid is not just a kid who plays too rough with toys. He intentionally *tortures* them. He's a little sociopath in the making, the sort who will likely soon move on to torturing animals and later evolve into a serial killer if he's not stopped, and that makes his character that much more frightening, and thus the whole movie that much more powerful.

We know nothing about why Sid is as bad as he is. If we knew, for example, that he was an abused kid, we'd no doubt see him in a more sympathetic light. As it is, he's simply rotten and thus easy to root against. And Sid's evil also significantly raises the stakes. Once our heroes are kidnapped (toynapped) by him, it's no longer just about the challenge of finding their way back to Andy. Sid ups the ante by making things truly a matter of life or death for our heroes.

Just for fun, here's *link to a list of the fifty best movie villains of all time.* See if you agree. *(http://www.timeout.com/newyork/film/ the-50-best-movie-villains-of-all-time)*

DEVELOPING CO-STARS, SUPPORTING PLAYERS and ORCHESTRATING CHARACTERS

Once you've identified some key qualities about your hero's character, who he is, how he sees the world and how he might need to grow, then you'll want to think about orchestrating the rest of your characters around him. You want to give him things to play off of, people to argue with, supporting players with differing world views and contrasting strengths and weaknesses.

You don't want to get lazy when it comes to filling out your supporting cast. Don't just make them stock or go for the first, most obvious generic characterization that comes to mind;

instead strive to make each character as distinct and original as possible.

We've all seen the gay best friend, the crude belching fat guy, the persnickety boss, the mean girl, ad nauseam. Instead, you want to give your supporting characters their own "particularity." Give them their moments, even think about giving them their own small character arcs. Jonah Hill as a dense would-be buyer of Elton John glam boots in *The 40-Year-Old Virgin* registers as a persistent kid who doesn't understand why he can't buy the boots straight from Trish's eBay store. And her patience with his thick-headedness underscores her kindness.

Opposites Attract

As you populate your script with supporting players and/or co-stars, again think about creating characters who personify opposing personality traits to play off your hero and one another: selfish versus generous, optimist versus pessimist, naif versus cynic, uptight versus easy-going, intellectual versus street smart. I find I like to play with the duality of romantic versus the cynic (probably because I'm a bit of both). By playing with duality and contrast and having opposites rub up against each other, you can get more juice and personality out of each of your characters.

Examples of Opposites:

- *Toy Story:* Woody is very down to earth, and Buzz is quite literally a spaceman.

- *The 40-Year-Old Virgin:* There's the total player/hound dog in Jay, the wounded romantic in David, the stoner goofball in Seth Rogen's Cal and the sweet virgin in Andy. And the contrast in the woman: Leslie Mann's neurotic drunk driver, the wacky women in the speed dating session, and Jane Lynch as his quirkily predatory boss all help set off the normalcy, warmth and sweetness of Catherine Keener's Trish.

- *Thelma & Louise:* We have the somewhat world-weary adult in Louise contrasted with the naive child in Thelma—until Thelma begins to change and come into her own power.

- *The King's Speech:* The warmth and informality of Logue's character and his family life is contrasted with the rigidity and coldness in much of Bertie's life and his extended family of origin.

- *Sideways:* Miles is an intellectual, morose, neurotic over-thinker; his best friend Jack is a reckless, narcissistic hedonist.

- *Bridesmaids:* The struggling everywoman in Annie contrasts with jaded housewife in Rita, the naive innocent in Becca, and the privilege and seeming perfection personified in Helen.

A couple of vintage examples:

- *Moonstruck:* Cher's two suitors, brothers Johnny and Ronnie Camerieri are opposites: Johnny is a stodgy, cautious mama's boy and Ronnie is reckless, passionate and "alive" and brings these qualities out in Cher.

- *Butch Cassidy and the Sundance Kid:* The optimist in Butch contrasts with the pessimist in Sundance.

Orchestrating your characters this way allows you to explore varying viewpoints, to create believable conflict and to play with philosophical questions. You effectively get to have your own personal debating society, and by putting words in opposing characters' mouths can argue and explore various points of view. And, because drama is conflict, this sort of contrast makes for more compelling storytelling, more friction, and more distinctive voices for your characters.

A WORD ABOUT ENSEMBLE PIECES:

True ensemble pieces are relatively rare, and writing one can be tricky. I would even argue that most of what might seem on the surface to be ensemble movies still do have one main character, the one through whose eyes we see the story, the one with whom the story begins and ends, the one who gets the most screen time and the one who changes the most.

Still, some films really do spread their focus fairly equally. A few examples include *Little Miss Sunshine, Love Actually, The Best Exotic Marigold Hotel* and *Spotlight*. One characteristic that distinguishes these movies as ensembles is that we typically meet all of the relevant players, all of the "leads," in the opening sequence.

Another important characteristic of an ensemble is that the players all have essentially the same goal and are dealing with variations of the same problem. In the case of *Little Miss Sunshine*, the challenge is getting Olive to the beauty pageant in California as each character faces a life crisis en route; in *Love Actually*, the struggle is to find and keep love; in *Marigold Hotel*, it's getting older, facing limited finances, moving to India and wondering what to do with the rest of their lives; and in *Spotlight*, it's exposing the Catholic Church's priest-pedophile scandal.

Finally, if the story that you're most eager to tell is genuinely an ensemble piece, then you should by all means write it, but I would caution you that it can be considerably more challenging to effectively service the goals, wants, needs, and character arcs of a multitude of players in less than two hours than it is to focus primarily on those of one main character. Things can easily start to feel scattered and perfunctory if you're not careful, so be sure to take the above-discussed criteria into account.

BUILDING CHARACTER(S) PART II TAKEAWAYS

1. The villain can be a key character and, if you have one, plays an important role in bringing your hero to his full true potential.

2. We typically know little of a villain's backstory.

3. Some of the scariest villains don't necessarily seem that way on the surface, at least not initially. If you have a villain, think about bringing a level of complexity to him, don't just make him mustache twirling or chainsaw juggling. Strive to figure out what his greatest hidden insecurity might be and exploit that.

4. Supporting players should provide contrast to the hero. Think in terms of orchestrating opposites and giving each character his own distinctive voice.

5. Writing an ensemble piece can be a challenge. Two tests of whether or not a story is a true ensemble are that screen time is divided pretty equally among all the players, and that all the characters are in pursuit of the same general goal.

BUILDING CHARACTER(S) PART II WORKSHEET:

1. Do you have a specific villain or antagonist whom your hero is going up against? Some stories do, some don't, but if yours does, you'll want this character to be as formidable as possible.

2. Does your villain represent a substantial enough threat to the hero and the hero's achievement of his goal to force the hero to a higher realization of himself?

3. Are your supporting players distinct? Have you given each his own unique character and voice?

4. If you're writing an ensemble piece, and thus dividing screen-time substantially among all the players, is everyone in pursuit of roughly the same goal?

STRUCTURALLY SPEAKING: LITTLE MISS SUNSHINE

READ: *LITTLE MISS SUNSHINE* Screenplay
(http://www.dailyscript.com/scripts/LITTLE_MISS_SUNSHINE.pdf)

Written by: Michael Arndt

Little Miss Sunshine is that rare example of a genuine ensemble piece. It's honestly hard to say which character in this film is the lead. I think the family, collectively, is real the star of the movie. Together, the family members pursue a common goal, and the family, as a unit, grows as a result. We meet each member of it before the main credits are over, and the following scene happens at the dinner table, again with everyone gathered in one place.

So, what does this mean for our structural analysis purposes? I don't mean to throw a wrench in the works of everything I've been covering for the past nine chapters. In fact, I believe that in a strange way, this movie reinforces what I've said about a lead character and how one defining characteristic of the lead is that he's the one with the goal. And this is where the distinction lies: In a true ensemble piece, there isn't a single lead character. Instead, most scenes need to feature everyone in the ensemble, and all the players *ought to be in pursuit of a common goal.* If you're writing an ensemble—which I would not advise you do on a first script, by the way, but if you are—this is an important principle to keep in mind.

Each character may also have his own problems and his own other goals, but what holds the story together as an ensemble is that the characters are all working together, and conflicting with one another, in pursuit of a common goal and doing so in almost every scene. This factor alone demonstrates how relatively uncommon true ensembles are.

Here each character has a wound/struggle/goal/and arguably an arc:

- Greg Kinnear's Richard/Dad is bent on being a self-help guru and being a "winner," but he is anything but.

- Steve Carell's Uncle Frank has just tried to kill himself over a failed love affair.

- Dwayne, the teenage son played by Paul Dano, is so alienated that he's stopped speaking altogether and has the clearly defined goal of becoming a military pilot.

- Alan Arkin as Grandpa has been kicked out of his retirement home, but actually seems rather at peace with himself. Still, he's a bit at war with everybody else and is also, not so incidentally, a heroin addict.

- Toni Collette as Sheryl, the mom, is just desperately trying to hold this whole dysfunctional gang together and to deal with everyone else's problems. Internally, she is frantic about the family finances and what the hell her husband is going to do for a living.

- Abigail Breslin's 7-year-old Olive, who's the least troubled of any of them, is the one with the goal they all become caught up in pursuing.

Again, this is a road trip movie, thus there's a built-in sense of forward momentum.

Act I

Quick cross-cuts establish the status quo for each member of the family: Olive is enraptured, watching a beauty pageant on TV; Richard, the father, is teaching a workshop on winners and losers to a less-than-enthusiastic junior college audience; Dwayne is working toward his enlistment goal, doing push-ups; poor Sheryl is at the hospital picking up her brother, Frank, who is recovering from a suicide attempt; and Grandpa is snorting drugs. Life goes on.

Arriving home with a fast food bucket of chicken, Sheryl works to get dinner laid out and everyone to the table.

The **Inciting Incident** is the phone call that comes in regarding Olive's suddenly being made eligible for the Little Miss Sunshine competition. The message is initially played back at 8 minutes into the film, but everyone in the family, Dad in particular, is so preoccupied with his own agenda that no one realizes this bolt from the blue has struck when it does, so the news is a bit delayed. Regardless, this message is the cause for all that follows, and the "if only" standard applies: If only that other little girl hadn't been disqualified from the pageant, none of this would ever have happened.

Plot Point #1:

Dad, ever on-topic regarding winners and losers, asks an ecstatic Olive if she intends to win the competition? When she answers in the affirmative, he announces, "We're goin' to California!" And we cut to them all loaded into the VW bus together.

Act II: Obstacles/Murphy's Law/Character Evolution

After Plot Point #1, the story literally takes off in a new direction as they all hit the road for California. They encounter a variety of obstacles en route, the first of which is that the clutch in the van breaks down and they have to all pull together (or actually push together) in order to keep moving forward. They must work as a team, and it's the first real moment of connection and collective happiness for them.

There are plenty more ups and downs in Act II, the greatest of which is that Grandpa overdoses and dies (exactly at the **Midpoint**, page 55, of a 110-page script). But desperate times call for desperate measures, so they figure out how to outsmart the petty bureaucrats at the hospital, steal away with his body hidden in the back of the van, and keep going.

(Side Note: Personally, I have a bit of a problem with this sequence. It just seemed too hard to buy that they wouldn't quit and go home, and there seems to be very little real grief. I mean I realize he was old, and their continuing to the pageant is ostensibly justified because "it's what Grandpa would have wanted," but still... he's *Grandpa*. It all seemed to turn a corner tonally a little too far into farce for me at this point. But, hey, Arndt got away with it and got an Oscar for his troubles, so what do I know?)

Anyway, there's also Dwayne's meltdown when he's devastated to discover that he's colorblind and thus can never be a pilot, another trauma that again threatens to scuttle the whole trip. But one way or another, they come together for Olive's sake and manage to keep moving forward.

By the skin of their teeth, they just barely make it to California and the pageant in time for Olive to be eligible to compete, but not before encountering yet more difficulty in simply finding the entrance to the hotel and in the form of a pissy pageant official who insists they're too late to participate. But even that obstacle is finally overcome, and now they take a good look around...

Plot Point #2:
And all take in the scene: the ridiculously overly-made-up little girls with their crazy elaborate costumes and their frantic stage mothers, and they realize that Olive, this sweet, plain, quite literally unadulterated kid, is in completely over her head. They recognize what she's really up against and how ill-suited she actually is to the task. Sheryl and Richard argue over the fact that she's not going to win, and he doesn't want to see her lose. Dwayne weighs in as well, insisting that Olive shouldn't be subjected to this, that "she's not a beauty queen."

ACT III

Despite the realities on the ground, Sheryl makes the tough call to forge ahead and let her participate, insisting she's earned this opportunity. When Olive finally appears onstage, amid all these ridiculously over-sexualized little girls, she stuns the room by performing an outrageous, enthusiastic, down and dirty strip club-inspired dance routine. Everyone in the family is shocked, but also elated by the genuine joie-de-vivre she exudes. When appalled pageant organizers try to force her off the stage, they all, led by Dad, defiantly join her there and dance together.

The Collective Character Arc:

Over the course of the movie everyone in the family loses something: Richard doesn't get his book deal; Frank sees he will never win his lost love back; Dwayne learns that he's color blind and thus will never be a fighter pilot; Grandpa is dead, and Olive is not going home with the crown of Little Miss Sunshine. And yet it is still a "feel-good movie" with a happy ending, because what they *do* ultimately get is the love and support of one another; they get what they need. As they rally together on Olive's behalf, they all momentarily give up whatever is preoccupying them; they give up their self-involvement and myopic focus on their own problems as they come together for her.

And thus, they are a team and a family and that's what matters most, as the movie ends on a happy note with them all dancing together, surrounding and supporting Olive.

> *"You can't always get what you want. But if you try sometimes, well you might find, you get what you need."*
>
> ~ The Rolling Stones

CHAPTER ELEVEN
WRITING THE SCENE

> *"I know it's crazy, but I just feel like I got a knack for this shit."*
>
> ~ Thelma Dickinson, after she robs the liquor store in *Thelma & Louise*, and one of my all-time favorite lines of dialogue.

CREENPLAYS ARE ABOUT STRUCTURE, AS it's extremely important in terms of keeping your story on track. But obviously each of the three acts is composed of individual pieces, and these pieces are the scenes.

Each scene should have a purpose in either further delineating character or moving the plot forward and, ideally, both. Writing a script is like stringing beads together; each bead is self-contained but also critically connected to the one on either side of it and to the whole. To justify its inclusion in your screenplay, a scene needs a good dramatic reason for being in terms of how it fits into the big picture and the overall story. And, just like a good journalist, you want to impart the who, what, where, when and, most important, the why of a scene.

Thus, as you string your scenes together, it's most effective if they can form a sort of cause and effect chain, where one is logically connected to and pushing into the next. Remember the advice from Trey Parker and Matt Stone about the words you want to be able to put between your scenes: "therefore" or "but," not simply "and then."

ON THE PAGE - THE SPECIFIC ELEMENTS THAT MAKE UP A SCENE:

These elements include:

- the slugline, which establishes the time and place of the scene

- action description

- the character's name

- dialogue

- any parenthetical information regarding how the line is to be delivered

- the occasional transition, (fade to, cut to, smash cut to, etc.)

When you begin writing a scene, the first thing you'll want to establish is where and when it's happening. This is done via the slugline. (The following sample is taken from pages 104-105 of *Thelma & Louise*. Please note that these elements are not to be in boldface in the script; I've just made them bold here to illustrate the point.)

A slugline looks like this:

EXT. SIDE OF DESERT HIGHWAY - DAY

As you can see, it's written in all caps, and establishes whether the scene is taking place inside or outside, (INT. or EXT.), where exactly it's happening, and what time of day it is.

Next you'll most likely describe the setting, the things the camera sees, and/or the action the characters are engaged in. In this page from *Thelma & Louise*, an example of action looks like this:

Louise pulls the car off the road. The patrol car pulls up right behind them. The lights shine brightly in through the windows.

Then, you'll most likely want to add dialogue. The name of the character who is speaking is always in all caps and is centered on the page above whatever words are said, like this:

THELMA
Please, God, please don't let us get caught. Please, please, please....

You might want to use a parenthetical to describe the manner in which a character says something. This will go between the name and the dialogue they speak, as follows:

LOUISE
(friendly)
Hello, Officer. Is there a problem?

Finally, it used to be customary to write "CUT TO:" between scenes and "CONTINUED" on the bottom of any page in which a scene was split over two pages. Neither of these conventions is commonly used today. The introduction of a new slugline implies the "CUT TO," and CONTINUED is also implied, as it just sort of clutters the page. If, however, you want to create a very strong cut in your script, something called a smash cut, or have a reason for wanting to really emphasize a sudden cut and juxtaposition of images, you can still use "CUT TO:" between scenes. It is formatted in all caps on the far right hand margin of the page, like so:

CUT TO:

10 TIPS FOR SCENE CONSTRUCTION:

1. Why Am I Here?
You want to know the answer to this question regarding every scene in your script. Scenes not meant to be random or arbitrary moments in a character's life, but instead the key and essential ones necessary to tell your story.

---

2. Be Economical and Evocative

When it comes to writing scene description and introducing characters, the goal is to be as succinct yet as descriptive as possible. You don't want to get bogged down in too many details, but you do want be vivid. I've always loved Callie Khouri's description of Darryl, Thelma's dope of a husband in *Thelma & Louise*:

"DARRYL comes trotting down the stairs. Polyester was made for this man, and he's dripping in 'men's' jewelry. He manages a Carpeteria."

It's the tip of the iceberg, but you get the sense that there *is* an iceberg. Khouri has clearly carefully thought through who this guy is, and it is through these specific details in these three spare sentences that we are given a clear mental picture not only of what this guy looks like but also of who he is as a person.

Another example of a character description that I quite like is from the script for *Sideways*, regarding a character named Ken: "He exudes the quiet confidence of a successful businessman who played college football, takes expensive skiing and sailing vacations, and hasn't read a novel since high school." Ha. It's just one sentence, but it speaks volumes.

Also remember that directors generally don't want you to play set dresser. You want to set the scene, evoke what you want in the reader's mind's eye as economically as possible, and move on. My movie *Only You* was set in Italy, and though it's not a period piece, I knew I wanted it to look romantic and idealized; meaning that the audience wasn't meant to see graffiti on the streets, garbage workers on strike, etc. So, very early in the script, I described it as follows:

"It's not the real Italy, it's the Italy of memories and dreams."

And there, in one sentence, I'm pretty much done. Later on, as locations changed, I'd describe the place and set the scene when necessary, but only very briefly, as the overall tone and look had already been established.

3. Arrive Fashionably Late and Leave Early

Yes, it's like that party where you want to make a cool impression. Get into the scene at the last possible moment, then move on as soon as you've made your point. Avoid what I once heard a writer call "throat clearing and paper shuffling." Skip the pleasantries and chit chat and cut as closely as you can to the absolute core purpose of the scene. And then don't stick around, don't let the scene overstay its welcome.

There is a tendency to overwrite in the beginning, and this is fine. In fact, it's a good thing. You must give yourself permission to do this and even to write "badly" in order to feel free enough to get it all down. You don't want to be censoring yourself too much on a first draft.

But then, as you go back over your work and rewrite, you must be tough, see where you can cut the chaff and pare things down to their essence. The audience is sophisticated, and you'd be amazed at how much better a scene or a script will read when you simply cut out anything that isn't truly necessary.

This, by the way, is an ever on-going process. If you watch any DVD commentary, you'll usually see deleted scenes. The editing goes on at every stage, even after the money has been spent in production. Personally, I love a good cut. It's so satisfying to be able to give a friend a script, have him look at it with fresh eyes, then knock out even a line or two and thereby make a scene play better and the script feel tighter.

4. One Thing Leads to Another

Remember, cause and effect, cause and effect. You want to create a well-connected chain of events. You don't want your scenes to be disjointed or to feel random or arbitrary; they should connect to one another and build on one another as they progress.

5. "Do Not Bore Them"

This is a quote from Billy Wilder regarding the audience. Exposition, as I've mentioned before, is critical information, often backstory information, plot details, perhaps scientific or historical facts, etc., that the audience needs to be aware of in order to fully understand and appreciate the story. An obvious example is the information in *Argo* that's communicated via voice-over and various visuals in the opening moments of the film.

More often, it's information that is given by one character to another, upon which the audience effectively eavesdrops. It's an often necessary evil, but too much of it can be story death, as everything comes to a grinding halt while some character spells out all the facts we need to know. (Slight digression: I felt that the film *Inception* suffered tremendously from this, with Ellen Paige's seemingly endless expositional speeches. Clearly plenty of other people disagreed; that, as they say, is what makes horse-racing. But until you're in the league of writer/director Christopher Nolan, you don't want to take the risk of making your dialogue feel stilted or of putting people to sleep with endless reams of this stuff.)

Ideally, you bury the exposition as artfully as possible. You integrate it into a conflict scene, or you give the character some amusing bit of business to engage in while the expositional medicine goes down. Or maybe rather than have your hero yammer on, you give the job to some quirky supporting character.

6. Be Specific, not Generic

The more specific the detail, the better. Don't be generic. It's not red, it's fire engine red, or crimson, or cherry-colored, etc. The more specific you are, the more interesting and relatable your script will be for the reader, and the more real it will feel.

Even the smallest things, if they're specific, can lead people to better respond and relate to your material. In *Bridesmaids*, when Annie runs into Chris O'Dowd's friendly cop for the second time in a "convenience store," (which seems almost a wink at how "convenient" it is that she runs into him, but I digress), the writers shake things up in a tiny way: He's buying carrots. Carrots. Who buys carrots at a 7-Eleven? And they sit on the trunk of the car and eat carrots. They don't drink beer or eat Doritos. If you make the extra effort to make even the little details unexpected, your script will feel that much fresher.

7. Behavior Reveals Character

When it comes to relationships, a friend of mine is fond of saying "Watch what they do, not what they say." What they do will tell you who they are, and what their real priorities are. This is true of both fictional characters and the real people in our lives. From *Thelma & Louise*, here's more of Callie Khouri's description the first time we meet Darryl:

"Darryl is checking himself out in the hall mirror, and it's obvious he likes what he sees. He exudes over-confidence for reasons that never become apparent. He likes to think of himself as a real lady killer. He is making imperceptible adjustments to his over-moussed hair."

It's simple yet telling. Especially that little bit of business he's given to do with his hair.

Another example that amuses me is from the 1986 movie *Ruthless People*. In it, a sweet, law-abiding, mild-mannered couple who've been completely screwed over by Danny De Vito's despicable businessman decide to kidnap his shrill, obnoxious wife, played by Bette Midler, and hold her for ransom.

There's a scene in which the nice wife, played by Helen Slater, starts to doubt the wisdom of what she and her husband, Judge Reinhold, have done, and he forcefully reminds her that DeVito deserves this, that they've got to fight fire with fire and have to be ruthless! And as he's in the midst of making this impassioned speech, insisting that she toughen up, he's ever-so-gently picking up a tiny spider on a piece of paper so that he can carry it outside to freedom. That behavior tells you all you need to know about his true character.

Finally, remember to let your characters behave the way people actually do: often tentatively, not as though their every action and word is preordained. Put in little hesitations, small gestures of going forward, then sliding back. Allow the nuances of emotion, conflicting emotions, and the many currents that simultaneously ebb and flow in real people to surface in their words and behavior.

8. Build, Don't Repeat

Movies move. They are all about forward momentum. If you find yourself with a bunch of scenes that are effectively communicating the same information you've already communicated and covering ground you've already covered, you run the risk of boring your viewers. Audiences are savvy; always keep things moving ahead.

9. Befriend Your Reader

The action description portion of your script is the place where you get to speak directly to your reader. You're their guide to this imaginary world you've created, and this is where your voice can shine. Don't be perfunctory and just state the facts.

Remember, you're talking to another human being as you write your story. And readers are not only looking at content, they're also looking for style. Your style of writing, the way you communicate with the person on the other end of your script, can make you stand out and can lead to future work even if the subject matter of a particular screenplay is not something a specific producer is looking to buy.

This concept of voice can sometimes be slightly hard to grasp.

Take a look at some scripts and see exactly how the writers are communicating with the reader on the page. Two famous filmmakers known for their distinctive voices are Quentin Tarantino, (*Reservoir Dogs*, *Pulp Fiction*, *Inglourious Basterds*, *Django Unchained*, *The Hateful Eight*), and Shane Black, (*The Long Kiss Goodnight*; writer and director of *Kiss, Kiss, Bang, Bang*; *Iron Man 2*). Both have what I'd call a fairly macho style on the page and Black, in particular, got a lot of attention back in the heyday of big spec sales for his over-the-top, distinctively aggressive and cocky style. I'm not suggesting you mimic that. What I am suggesting is that you find your own voice—ironic, playful, confessional, cool, whatever it may be—and use it to your advantage. Write as if you're telling your story to a friend, one who gets it and gets you.

10. Beginning, Middle, End – And Don't Overdo It.

Just as your script will, ideally, have a beginning, middle and end with nothing superfluous, so should your scenes be constructed. They should have a beginning, middle and end and no flab in between. And when I say a beginning, middle and end, I mean more than that they start somewhere, go on for a while, and then stop someplace else. You want there to be a purpose to everything in the scene. You get in at the latest possible moment, do what you need to do, and then, having made your point, get out at the earliest opportunity.

In terms of length, scenes can be anywhere from just a few lines to multiple pages long, but I would not advise going over five pages for any one scene unless you have a *very* good reason.

Just to be contrary, a fairly recent example of a scene that does run much longer than normal is the opening of Aaron Sorkin's *The Social Network*, for which Sorkin took home the Oscar. Here I'm reminded of what a brilliant high school English teacher of mine once told a student who complained that he should be able to use run-on sentences because William Faulkner used them. The kid even pulled out a copy of *The Sound and the Fury* to illustrate his point. To which my teacher responded, "When you can write like William Faulkner, you can write like William Faulkner. Until then, you'll write the way I tell you to write." Well, when you can write like Aaron Sorkin, you can write like Aaron Sorkin. Until then, trust me on this, don't go over five pages per scene unless you have a very good reason.

SCENE WRITING TAKEAWAYS:

1. Each scene should fulfill a specific purpose in moving the story forward and/or further delineating character; ideally both.

2. You want to get into the scene at the latest moment possible, and out at the earliest moment possible.

3. Scenes should not be random snippets out of a character's life; they should help build the story and illuminate the characters in it.

4. You want to be able to insert the words "and therefore" or "but" between each of your scenes, not simply "and then." You want you scenes to connect and to build upon one another.

5. A script reader is looking at both the content of your script and its style. Your voice, the way you communicate with your reader on the page, is key. Try to take the reader into your confidence and even occasionally speak to him directly.

SCENE WRITING WORKSHEET:

1. For each scene, ask yourself what, specifically, is its purpose? What critical information is it conveying? Is it essential?

2. Is this the best possible way to convey that information?

3. How is this scene moving the story forward or further fleshing out character?

4. Am I repeating myself? Have I already communicated this information to the audience, or am I adding something new? This is another way of asking: is my story building?

5. Can each scene be connected to the one that came before it and the one that comes after it with the words "and therefore" or "but," not the words "and then."

6. Am I talking to my reader, taking him into my confidence as I write?

STRUCTURALLY SPEAKING: THELMA & LOUISE

READ: THELMA & LOUISE Screenplay
(http://www.pages.drexel.edu/~ina22/splaylib/Screenplay-Thelma_and_Louise.pdf)

Written by: Callie Khouri

For background on the film, READ: The Making of Thelma & Louise - The Ride of a Lifetime (http://www.vanityfair.com/news/2011/03/the-making-of-thelma-and-louise-201103)

I so love this movie. It's smart, funny, heartbreaking, empowering, suspenseful and gorgeous to look at. It really holds up, and all these years later still packs a punch.

According to screenwriter Callie Khouri, the script was a gift from the Muses. She came up with the core notion of "two women who go on a crime spree," didn't want them to be criminals, then worked backward to figure out what might drive two ordinary women to this extreme. (And, by the way, this was her first script and she won the Oscar for Best Screenplay. Not a bad beginning.)

Act I

Khouri's introduction of characters and establishment of the status quo is pretty brilliant. She effectively paints vivid mental pictures of these people with just a few strokes, just a few details, but manages to convey so much with just a few well-chosen words. There's a simplicity to her writing; she's not Jane Austen, but she doesn't need to be. She conjures each character— through description, body language and dialogue— clearly, succinctly, and often wittily.

And she really manages to make her people sound different

and specific, not only the leads, but also the supporting players, Darryl, Harvey Keitel's character of the investigator, Brad Pitt's JD, etc.

Inciting Incident: Their stopping at the country western bar and unknowingly meeting would-be rapist, Harlan, sets the stage and is the cause for all that follows. (11 minutes in.)

Plot Point #1:

Louise shoots and kills Harlan (22 minutes in). This is the action she takes to solve an immediate problem that then has unintended consequences.

Act II

Now they're outlaws on the run, and all sorts of unanticipated events, challenges and obstacles ensue. These include:

- Their meeting the hitchhiker, J.D.,and Thelma's subsequent sexual awakening

- Louise's come-to-Jesus meeting with, proposal from and subsequent breakup with her boyfriend, Jimmy

- J.D.'s stealing of their money — the **Midpoint**

- The women's decision to flee the country

- The cops closing in

Also, the characters start to evolve, especially Thelma. Some signs of her transformation:

- "How long 'til we're in goddamm Mexico?" (She's not going back.)

- She tells her husband to go fuck himself.

- She robs the convenience store and becomes ever more brazen.

- She literally takes the wheel of the car.

- They both start to look different, physically toughened, especially Thelma who started off all frilly and girly. By the end, they both wind up looking badass.

- She is the one who puts a gun to the head of the cop who stops them for speeding, then takes charge as she begins giving instructions to Louise, (take his gun, shoot the radio, etc.)

- She says that "something's crossed over" in her.

- She's the one who hangs up the phone on Keitel's character.

Character Arcs: This is very much a buddy movie, with two strong leads, but it is called **Thelma** & Louise. Thelma comes first. I think it's slightly more her movie, as she has the bigger, showier arc. She, much more than Louise, changes over the course of the story and begins to behave in new ways. In the beginning, Thelma is something of a child, Louise is the more world-weary adult. But by the end, their roles have almost reversed, with Thelma calling the shots.

Plot Point #2:

104 minutes in: I believe it's the conversation Louise has with Keitel's sympathetic cop in which he's understanding—he tells her that he knows what happened to her in Texas—but also that he has no choice but to charge them with murder. Thelma hangs up the phone as Louise is still talking to him, but we learn that they've been traced, and we also learn that Thelma's not so sure she can trust her best friend any more. The walls are closing in. Now they're really on the run. This is at 1 hour, 44 minutes into a 2 hour, 9 minute movie, so it's right on target with about 25 minutes remaining for Act III.

Act III

They come out of the low point of the conversation with Keitel when Louise reassures Thelma that she's not making any deals, not going back or giving her up. This is also when Thelma has her epiphany, realizes that "something's crossed over" in her, that she feels "awake" and knows she can't go back. And they have that funny, poignant conversation about their future in Mexico in which Louise reassures her, "We'll be drinkin' margaritas by the sea, Mamasita."

For the record, Act III does have a couple of elements that seem just slightly off track to me in an otherwise very tight script:

1. The harassment of the trucker seems to make them just a little unsympathetic as they go from victims to victimizers. Yes, he's a complete idiot and, yes, it does show them coming into their own power, but I found it somehow a little off-putting. Also, I couldn't help but think isn't this escapade slowing down their getaway to Mexico? I seem to remember hearing that Ridley Scott, the director, quite liked the blowing up of the truck and wanted to keep it.

2. The rasta guy on the bike blowing smoke into the trunk where the cop is stashed is all well and good and sort of amusing, and it's a very short bit, but structurally it seems off-track. I don't think this scene was actually in the script. I think it was something they came up with during the shoot, and just kind of couldn't resist.

But ultimately, no matter. Really I'm just nit-picking, as there's so much that's fantastic about this script and the narrative drive is so strong here we don't lose it.

One more thing I want to point out here is the subtle but effective use of backstory, the term for what has gone on in the lives of the characters before the story began, before we as the audience dropped in on them. In this case, what is clearly alluded to but quite never spoken outright is that Louise was raped in Texas. It informs the whole movie, especially her shooting of Harlan, but we're never hit over the head with it. The fact that it remains unspoken makes it, I think, that much more powerful and artful.

And so by the end, despite the choice they make to head over the cliff, we're still left with a sense of empowerment. (And I'm still kind of amazed that Khouri wasn't forced by the studio to change that ending.) Regardless, we still feel these women have claimed their own power and freed themselves from the shackles of their former lives. Khouri, when asked about the ending put it this way, "They don't die, they fly." Whether you fully buy that line of thinking or not, I think there's no denying that by the end of the movie, these women have taken the reins of their own lives.

CHAPTER TWELVE

PUTTING WORDS IN THEIR MOUTHS: DIALOGUE

"You have all the scenes. Just go home and word it in."

~ Samuel Goldwyn to Billy Wilder
and I.A.L. Diamond

WHEN YOU TELL PEOPLE YOU write screenplays for a living, sometimes those not familiar with the process will ask if you "make up all the words they say and everything?" Even if they even realize that there *is* a writer involved, they often imagine that writing the dialogue is all there is to it. You just put clever lines in people's mouths. They don't necessarily appreciate the fact that these words (and actions) reveal who these characters are as human beings and are connected to the overall plot and structure and story, which you've also pulled out of your own heart, mind and the thin air, and worked day and night to get down on paper with great effort. (Oops, might've slipped into Bitter Writer mode there. Deep breath....)

Okay, back to my point.

Writing dialogue can be challenging in that you want it to sound the way people actually talk, and yet you sort of don't. To again paraphrase Sydney Pollack in *Tootsie*, "They can see that in New Jersey!" We hear people talk all day long. What we're looking for is what I'd call heightened naturalism. And no matter how clever the exchange, if it doesn't have a structural reason for being there, either in revealing character or moving your story forward, it doesn't belong in your script. The last thing you want to do is let your characters just blather on merely for the hell of it, or simply to fill up pages.

When crafting dialogue, you want to be clear on what you're trying to communicate emotionally, character-wise and/or plot-wise, and then see if you can pare that down to its essence. Strive to jump in at the last possible moment and see if you can leave enough unsaid that the audience is invited to put things together for themselves. As Billy Wilder put it, "Let the audience add up two plus two. They'll love you forever."

10 TIPS FOR WRITING EFFECTIVE DIALOGUE:

1. And Your Point Is?

Dialogue is not just arbitrary chit chat, nothing is duller. You want to know the true purpose of each scene; how you are moving the story forward and/or telling us something new about the characters. That, to a large extent, can and should dictate your dialogue.

When you find yourself having trouble writing dialogue in a scene, the problem often lies in the deeper purpose of the scene, which is either unclear, structurally offtrack or unnecessary. Check these things, and if they're all in order, sometimes the easiest solution is not to get tied up in knots trying too hard to be clever or brilliant or profound, but to simply ask yourself, "What would somebody in this situation actually say?"

2. Vary the Voices in Your Head

Ideally, different characters should sound different from one another. Try to think in terms of each character's emotional core. When coming up with his "voice," consider the primary lens through which he sees the world. Is he a cynic? A romantic? A whiner? A stoner? A charmer? A liar? A victim? A bully? Sensitive? Angry? Charming? Pollyanna? Deviant? Cynical?

Smooth? Then ask yourself, how would someone with this sort of personality respond in this situation?

And again, think about orchestrating opposites. Can you pit an optimist against a pessimist? Juxtapose a neurotic with a hedonist? Not incidentally, this exercise allows you to give voice to different sides of your own personality. It allows you to debate an issue with yourself; to explore all sides of it and discover where your own truth lies.

3. Tip of the Iceberg

I sometimes think of dialogue as revealing the tip of the iceberg of a person's character and personality. You, as the writer, must be sure there *is* an iceberg beneath the surface. That is, you want to know who each person is deep down and what makes him tick, then reveal just that critical bit that lets the audience in on this in a shorthand way, that provides a glimpse of the bigger picture. This allows for more of that "two plus two" that can be so much more fun for the viewer.

Ideally you want to avoid what is called "on-the-nose" dialogue, the sort of brute dialogue one often hears in soap operas, in which everyone's always spelling out the situation and exposition in elaborate boring detail for the viewer. Instead, aim to be a little oblique, to use subtext, to be witty, or unexpected or just be bracingly honest. This principle of revealing just the tip of the iceberg also works in terms of behavior. Little things can mean and reveal a lot, in movies as in life, and it's fun for an audience to deduce a larger truth about a character from a seemingly small action or gesture.

> *"Don't tell me the moon is shining; show me the glint of light on broken glass."*
>
> ~ Anton Chekhov

4. Don't Waste My Time

Once you're clear on the purpose of a scene, you need to get to that purpose as quickly as possible. As Shakespeare advised, "Brevity is the soul of wit." "When in doubt, cut it out." (I don't think that second one was his, but it's still a valid point.)

5. Drama is Conflict

If life is all beautiful and peaceful and everybody's getting on fabulously, that's terrific in reality, but in a movie, it's death. It's fine to have a scene or two, particularly in the beginning, in which everything is grand, but pretty soon something had better go wrong for somebody. Matthew Weiner, the creator of *Mad Men*, has said, "Super-confident people with no problems and great marriages and great parenting are not good entertainment."

Let your characters argue. Conflict can be on a grand scale: a war, the invasion of aliens, etc., or on an intimate, interpersonal scale as in *Sideways*, but it's got to be there in some form pretty much every step of the way. You need to know who wants what out of each scene, and somebody had better always be wanting something and usually going up against something or somebody else in the process of trying to get it.

6. Listen Carefully

As Hemingway advised, listen to the way people actually speak. They don't always speak in full, grammatically correct sentences. In fact, most of the time they don't, and your characters don't need to either. People hesitate, they dance around a subject, go at each other, leave things unsaid, etc. On the other hand, this *is* meant to be drama. You want a certain amount of verisimilitude yet, ideally, it all ought to be more interesting than real life, otherwise people wouldn't need to bother going to movies in the first place.

7. Be "Entertaining"

Wit is like a get-out-of-jail-free card. You can make virtually any sort of exposition fly if you're clever and witty enough about it. As long as an audience is being entertained, they'll swallow all sorts of information and hokum and contrivance and not blink an eye.

Of course there are some movies with subject matter so serious that humor might seem out of place and you might have to be careful with tone, but it's almost always welcome. Funny doesn't have to mean silly, broad or slapstick; you can be wry or ironic, satirical or darkly comic. Even a movie as violent as *Pulp Fiction,* or one that deals with subject matter as serious as WWII and the Nazis *(Casablanca)* or terrorists *(Argo)* benefits from comic relief. And when it comes to the necessary medicine of exposition, wit is like that proverbial spoonful of sugar.

8. Be Unexpected
Sometimes it's helpful to ask yourself what's the most obvious thing somebody would say in this situation, and then turn that 180 degrees on its head.

9. Write Between the Lines; Use Subtext
Subtext is quite literally what it sounds like. It is what is going on beneath the actual text; what is technically unsaid but is being communicated "between the lines." People often don't come right out and say what's on their minds. It's too scary, too soul-baring, too confrontational. So they tiptoe around the subject. The more you, as a writer, are able to communicate what you want to communicate without spelling everything out— to not be "on-the-nose" about it—the more artful and sophisticated your writing will be. It will up the perception of your game.

> *"Subtleties are fine, as long as we make them obvious."*
>
> ~ Billy Wilder

Subtext Examples:

Argo: An effective use of subtext in this film occurs when Sahar, the family's housekeeper, comments to the ambassador's wife regarding the diplomats hiding out in their home, "Your Canadian friends never go out." We know exactly what she's getting at and, just in case we don't, we immediately cut to the wife telling her husband, "Sahar knows." This is a textbook example of making your subtleties obvious. The audience gets the pleasure of putting things together for themselves and then, for anyone who missed it, there's the punchline that confirms: "Sahar knows."

This scene is later bookended with a smart, tension-filled scene in which Sahar is being questioned by a suspicious man on the street, and which reveals to us her true loyalties. She doesn't give the diplomats up and instead lies to the man that the "guests" have been there for only two days. This scene also underscores the pressure she's under as an Iranian, the dangerous position the Canadians and Americans have put her in.

Sideways: A scene I love in *Sideways* is the one where Miles and Maya find themselves alone together for the first time in Stephanie's kitchen and Maya asks him why he's so into Pinot Noir. While ostensibly enumerating all the reasons that he loves this particular type of wine, what he's really (subconsciously) talking about is himself.

MAYA
Can I ask you a personal question?

MILES
(bracing himself)
Sure.

MAYA
Why are you so into Pinot? It's like a
thing with you.

Miles laughs at first, then smiles wistfully at the question. He searches for the answer in his glass and begins slowly.

MILES

> I don't know. It's a hard grape to grow. As you know. It's thin-skinned, temperamental, ripens early. It's not a survivor like Cabernet that can grow anywhere and thrive even when neglected. Pinot needs constant care and attention and in fact can only grow in specific little tucked-away corners of the world. And only the most patient and nurturing growers can do it really, can tap into Pinot's most fragile, delicate qualities. Only when someone has taken the time to truly understand its potential can Pinot be coaxed into its fullest expression. And when that happens, its flavors are the most haunting and brilliant and subtle and thrilling and ancient on the planet.

He's ostensibly talking about wine, but beneath the surface what he's really giving us is a glimpse into his soul. If only someone took the time to "cultivate" him, they would be amply rewarded.

10. Show, Don't Tell: No Words at All

Before there were "talkies" there were silent movies. In the beginning, most information was communicated visually, but now that we're so accustomed the luxury of dialogue we sometimes forget the power of silence.

The last scene from Lost in Translation, Sofia Coppola's beautiful and poignant meditation on travel, love and feeling adrift in Tokyo, is a perfect example of how effective it can be.

Bill Murray and Scarlett Johansson play strangers of different generations who find themselves with time their hands in the same hotel in a foreign land. He's there for work and is estranged from his wife; she's feeling distant from her new husband; and neither speaks the language. Their relationship is nuanced, it's really much more platonic than romantic, but there are many currents in the tide. The two seem to be, for lack of a better phrase, kindred souls.

After having had a falling out toward the end of the film, one that threatens to poison the warm, genuine connection that has been forged between them over just a few days, they have one last moment together that's so private that even we, in the audience, are not privy to it.

Coppola shoots from a distance, so that we don't quite hear what Murray whispers in Johansson's ear after they run into each other and say goodbye on the street. And something about this scene is so moving. I can't imagine any words we could've heard there that would have been as powerful as seeing the two of them privately, quietly share this final moment of understanding and farewell.

DIALOGUE TAKEAWAYS:

1. When it comes to dialogue, less is usually more. Make all your words count and don't overdo it.

2. Try to avoid on-the-nose dialogue. The vast majority of the time the audience is already ahead of you and, regardless, it's boring. Don't just tell us about someone or something, show us.

3. Strive to vary and orchestrate the voices of your characters.

4. See if you can work some subtext into your scenes. Do as Billy Wilder and Andrew Stanton advise and make your audience put two and two together, don't just hand them

four. But remember to be sure to leave enough breadcrumbs for people to follow and be able to add things up.

5. Sometimes silence can be more powerful than any dialogue.

DIALOGUE WORKSHEET:

1. Are your characters speaking in distinct voices?

2. Have you given them things to argue about and made it a fair fight?

3. Is there any place where your dialogue is too on-the-nose? Can you tweak it to make it a little subtler, a little slyer?

4. Can you get someone to read your work aloud? If nothing else, record yourself reading it and listen to the way it sounds.

5. Experiment with subtext, even try using no dialogue at all if it's appropriate to the scene.

6. Cut the chaff. A small edit can often make a big difference in how well a scene plays.

STRUCTURALLY SPEAKING: THE KING'S SPEECH

READ: *THE KING'S SPEECH Screenplay*
(http://www.pages.drexel.edu/~ina22/splaylib/Screenplay-Kings_Speech_The.pdf)

Written by: David Seidler

WATCH: *David Seidler, writer, on his creative process.*
(https://www.youtube.com/watch?v=Z43xej7evbk)

This is a dialogue-heavy film; there's not a lot of action, it could almost be a play. Still, plenty happens and the dialogue is smart, sophisticated and subtly witty, and the story is quite compelling, particularly because it's true. Also, the leads are very sympathetic and well drawn, and the suspense maintained throughout because we know what's at stake. All of these elements combine to make it a wonderfully effective and entertaining drama.

The script is also a brilliant example of the Billy Wilder adage about subtleties being made obvious. There are many subtleties here; the script gives its audience credit for intelligence. It lets moviegoers put things together for themselves, and yet what's going on, in terms of both plot and characters, is always very clear.

Lionel Logue, the speech therapist, functions as both an ally and something of an antagonist in the film. Once he meets Bertie, the Duke of York, Logue graciously but firmly counters the royal and his insecure imperiousness line for line. He quickly proves that despite their differences in class, he's an equal.

Note that there's nothing extraneous in the dialogue between them; everything Logue says has a purpose, even something as seemingly inconsequential as "Cuppa tea?" There's a method to his madness. The two of them initially verbally spar in a very proper, polite English way.

What Bertie wants, his external goal, is established clearly and early on: to lose his stammer and be able to speak clearly. He doesn't yet realize that he has an internal emotional need as well, to come to terms with the traumas of his childhood, or that the two things are connected.

ACT I

The movie opens with a "teaser" that immediately tells you what the protagonist's dilemma is. In a variation on Michael Arndt's theory about the movie opening with the hero doing the thing he loves most, here we meet Bertie, the Duke of York, doing the thing he most despises—trying to speak in public and failing miserably. From a certain angle, however, he's also trying to do the thing he most wants to be able to do: to fully express himself and thus honorably represent the monarchy.

Inciting Incident: Page 10 - The bolt from the blue happens to both Lionel and to Bertie when Bertie's wife Elizabeth hires Logue to work with her husband, unbeknownst to him. In a sense, the bolt from the blue happens directly to Logue and sort of in-absentia to Bertie, but it still happens. And interestingly, once it does, the next four pages are spent on Logue: introducing his family life, which is then juxtaposed, contrasted and paralleled with Bertie's.

Then there are the scenes illustrating Logue's mostly unsuccessful acting aspirations, and it isn't until page 19 that Bertie meets Lionel for the first time. In such a short script—just 92 pages—I find it it is interesting that Seidler gets away with this degree of initial focus on the second banana. In a sense, this is a buddy movie and thus it has a slightly more complex structure. Still, Bertie is clearly the main character. It is, after all, called *The King's Speech*, not *The Speech Therapist Gets a Really Famous Client*.

Regardless, Bertie shows up at Logue's office, albeit reluctantly, and they spar, meeting each other line for line. Logue will not be intimidated. They are equals in his office and each is formidable in his own way. But I don't think this first visit is Plot Point #1. Bertie is half-hearted initially, he's been dragged there by his wife, he's not committed, so the tension and pressure on him continue to build in Act I.

Shortly after he storms out of Logue's office, there is the exposition conveyed by his father, the king, regarding his brother David's dalliances, the changing place of the monarchy, and the geopolitical threats the country faces. What is at stake is established and, because they are royalty, the burden is great. It's not just Bertie's personal functionality or his ability to support his family that's at stake— it's potentially the fate of the nation, and for that matter of the free world. His brother is irresponsible and ill-suited for the job, and there are storm clouds on the horizon in the form of Nazi Germany.

The pressure is further increased when we again we see Bertie fail at speaking in front of his father and seem to shrink from the duty. All alone after being goaded by his father, Bertie plays the record he'd recorded in Logue's office and, for the first time, hears himself speaking clearly; then we immediately cut to him and his wife back again at Logue's office.

Plot Point #1, page 29
The moment of his listening to his clear voice and the immediate cut back to Logue's office make for a very nice Plot Point #1 and shift into Act II. This transition is an especially good illustration of cause and effect linkage between scenes, and of showing, not telling.

Now Bertie has really taken some action, and he dives in in earnest. He thinks his problem is his stutter and, despite his years of suffering, still believes the solution will be a relatively minor matter of mastering the proper vocal exercises.

He shows up impatient to be "cured," but will ultimately learn that his dilemma goes far deeper than the way he speaks; that it's a symptom of a larger issue. Soon he is forced confront the wounds of his childhood. His having to ultimately admit and somehow make peace with the fact that he was bullied, abused and suffered as a child is one of the unanticipated consequences of his action. And finding the courage to do so will prove to be his greatest obstacle en route to his ultimate goal.

ACT II

The story has turned a corner into a new direction, and we're fully into Act II. You can see how Act I was the set up, and how now the dynamic between the two men has changed; they're becoming a team, now they're really working together.

Also, Bertie starts behaving in new ways, opening up, little by little, to Logue's process and teachings. So there are hills and valleys in terms of Bertie's personal progress, in terms of the relationship between him and Lionel, and in terms of the other issues in his family and in the world at large.

With the death of his father, Bertie starts to open up a little more and Logue (and we) get a window into his childhood and its deprivations; how he suffered and has internalized the abuse and the minimalization of his feelings. This getting down to the nitty-gritty, as Bertie's starts delving into and describing his childhood pain, is the **Midpoint** of the film. It happens at pages 45 and 46, (of a 92-page script), and after this information is brought to Bertie's consciousness and shared with Logue, nothing will be the same.

The ante is upped further when not only does his father die but his brother David, the rightful heir to the throne, falls for an American divorcee and seems utterly disinterested in his royal duties (an unexpected twist).

The pressure ultimately causes Bertie to lash out at Logue when Logue tries to be helpful and suggests that Bertie possibly could be king, that he could potentially outshine his brother. Bertie reacts with shock and anger at the impudence of this suggestion, and this leads to an estrangement between the two.

Meantime, war with Germany is brewing. Murphy's Law is at work in a big way as crisis is piled upon crisis. David announces he's going to marry Wallis Simpson and abdicates. Talk about life's curveballs! And now the job, with its immense responsibilities and pressure, is truly Bertie's.

Plot Point #2, the lowest point, page 70

At that first crucial test, with the weight of the world upon him and without Logue to support him, Bertie again crumbles and fears that as a result, the public will despise him and he will fail miserably in his duty to the country.

ACT III

But now, with the loving support of his wife, he recommits to his goal, takes action, seizes the reins and initiates a reconciliation with Logue. It goes well, but the larger problem/goal still looms. The battle may be won, but the war, quite literally here, isn't over.

Britain goes to war with Germany over the invasion of Poland, and thus the stakes are raised further still. Now it's not just about Bertie; the fate of the free world is on his shoulders, and he feels enormous pressure. He doubts himself again (two steps forward, one step back) and in another argument with Logue, he has his epiphany when he yells that he has a right to be heard, that he has a voice. This is his character arc.

Now, as he rehearses the speech to the nation, we see the progress he has made, but the suspense is still maintained as we've seen him choke at this a number of times.

Page 92: Thus, it's a very satisfying resolution when, with Logue and his wife at his side, he manages to rise to the occasion and successfully speak clearly to the public as their new king. And the filmmakers are forgiven for the neatness with which all is wrapped up because this is (one assumes) how it actually happened. Not only does Bertie evolve personally, we're also left with the impression that the monarchy, and thus the by extension the free world, is in good, responsible, confident hands.

CHAPTER THIRTEEN

THE BUSINESS OF SHOWBIZ, PART ONE
& HOW TO WIN AN OSCAR

> *"I'd like to have money. And I'd like to be a good writer. Those two can come together, and I hope they will, but if that's asking too much, I'd rather have the money."*
>
> ~ Dorothy Parker

So, YOU'VE SLAVED OVER YOUR script. You've written and rewritten, proofread and rewritten some more. You've spent many a sleepless night wrestling with seemingly intractable story problems, only to wake up the next day and realize the real problem isn't in Act III, it's in Act I.

You've gone back to the drawing board innumerable times, run your work by friends and lovers and the barista at Starbucks, and made it as good as you possibly can. And now the moment of truth has arrived. It's time to send your little brainchild out on its own into the cold, cruel world. But the world of Hollywood isn't really as bad as you've heard, right?

Of course not.

It's worse.

Buckle up, because here's the reality: The movie business can be cruel, heartbreaking, obscenely unfair, ugly, vicious and downright soul-stealing. You sold so far? Trust me, the rudeness, nepotism, back-stabbing, phoniness, thievery and sheer mind-boggling ruthlessness you've seen depicted in satirical movies about showbiz are proverbial kid's stuff compared to what actually goes on on a daily basis. I tell my friends the film *The Player* is a documentary.

Show business is also still shamefully sexist and racist. These issues were again recently brought to greater public attention with the 2016 Academy Awards #OscarsSoWhite protests and the Sony Pictures hack in 2014 which revealed, among other things, that actresses working for Sony were routinely paid less than male actors of equal star stature. The hack also again proved the validity of a phrase of a writer friend of mine was fond of repeating regarding agents and other suits: *"These people are not your friends."* Heck, if the Sony situation demonstrates anything, it goes to show these people aren't even Angelina Jolie's friends. Or each other's for that matter.

According to a 2015 study conducted by the University of California, Los Angeles, the top executives at major Hollywood film studios are *94 per cent white and 100 per cent male.* **(http://www. bunchecenter.ucla.edu/wp-content/uploads/2015/02/2015-Hollywood-Diversity-Report-2-25-15.pdf)** A 2015 article in *LA Weekly* titled "How Hollywood Keeps Out Women" covered the problem of sexism in greater detail. Reporter Jessica P. Ogilvie contacted the following Big Six Studio executives to confirm their film counts between Jan. 1, 2010, and Dec. 31, 2014—and the number of those films directed by women. Warner Bros. and Universal responded. The other executives had no comment, did not respond or were said to be too busy, but Ogilvie managed to ferret out the following statistics:

Warner Bros.: Kevin Tsujihara, chairman and CEO :
According to the Internet Movie Database, Warner Bros. produced 72 films from 2010 through 2014. One was directed by a woman. A Warner Bros. representative said via email, "WB released 72 films ... 53 of which we produced; 19 were only distributed by WB. Of those 53 films produced and distributed by WB, three were directed by women."

Twentieth Century Fox chairman-CEO James Gianopulos and film studio co-chairman Stacey Snider:
Twentieth Century Fox, 20th Century Fox Animation and FOX 2000 produced 45 films. One was directed by a woman.

NBC Universal, Ronald Meyer, vice chairman:
Combined, Universal and Focus Features produced 101 films. Five were directed by women and one was co-directed by a woman.

Paramount Pictures: Brad Grey and Rob Moore, the chairman-CEO and vice chairman, respectively.
Paramount produced 51 films. One was directed by a woman; one was co-directed by a woman.

Sony Pictures: Michael Lynton, CEO.
Sony's largest studios, Columbia and TriStar, produced 62 films. One was directed by a woman.

Walt Disney Studios: Alan Bergman, president.
Disney Studios and Disney Animation produced 52 films. Two had women as co-directors.

This despite the fact that the numbers of men and women coming out of film school are relatively equal.

Creating and maintaining a career in entertainment has always been an uphill battle for everyone; for women, anyone over forty, and people of color—or God forbid any combination thereof—it's Everest. A friend once calculated the odds of someone becoming a professional screenwriter and figured that, statistically speaking, it would be easier to become a professional baseball player. I once worked with a woman who was fond of saying "Hollywood always finds a way to break your heart." (She was, by the way, especially adept at doing this to people.) I have found all of these things, on the whole, to be true.

And here's more good news: None of that's probably ever going to change. If you don't believe me, read Budd Schulberg's classic novel *What Makes Sammy Run?* written about the movie business in 1941 and see how much the dynamics remain the same. *Plus ça change.*

So if you're going to survive this game, you have to somehow find a way to make your peace with the realities on the ground. Right or wrong (and obviously I think it's wrong, but—) it is the nature of the beast. The cold, hard fact of the matter is that the odds are enormously stacked against you every step of the way. But, hey, I shouldn't sugarcoat it, right?

Ok, so that's the bad news. (Well, some of it anyway.) *But....*

This business can also be incredibly exciting, inspiring, rewarding, fascinating, lucrative and extraordinarily fun. And one of the things I love best about it is that anything can happen. I am living proof. After three years as Vice President of Creative Affairs to director Sydney Pollack, and working seven days a week at it, I was driven out of my dream job by a woman so cunningly manipulative she could've given Machiavelli pointers.

But although she set out to destroy me, the truth is she wound up unintentionally doing me a great favor, because she drove me to become a writer. Yep, I am the poster child for loving your enemies because they can be instruments of your destiny. She was my own personal antagonist, and her behavior was my own Inciting Incident. The position she forced me into left me no choice but to take action to try to solve my dilemma.

At the time I was devastated and unemployed, but I clung to the fact that the one thing no one could take from me was what I had learned while working there. So I kept writing.

I got an agent off the first script I wrote (at night, in three months, while I was still working for the company). That script was called *Dog Meets Cat* and, with it, my agent got me one meeting: I landed the job and got a small option to write a treatment—a story outline—for an animation company called Hanna-Barbera.

This little assignment then got me into the Writers Guild of America and provided me with a year's worth of health insurance. And a little over a year later, I sold the second screenplay I ever wrote for $1 million up front. It became the film *Only You*.

When that surreal moment occurred, when my attorney and agent called to tell me they'd closed my deal for that staggering amount, they asked me if there was anything else I wanted. In my daze, I managed to find the presence of mind to ask if I got to go to Italy (the story was set there.) My attorney responded, "Do you want to go to Italy?" "Um, yes, I believe I do." The following summer, I traveled to Italy on the company dime during the shoot, got to hang out with Robert Downey Jr. and sip limoncello while watching the sun set over a cobalt sea in Positano. *So there.*

HOW TO KEEP GOING

I am often asked, especially by those who have become discouraged, how did you do it? How did you manage to succeed at this? How did you keep going? The closest I can come to an answer is to say you just *keep at it*.

If you want it enough, you keep at it. You find ways, as the Muppets taught us, over, under, through. You have to want whatever you want more than you fear and abhor all the truly awful things that almost inevitably come with the territory. You have to be willing to persevere long past the point you ever thought you might be able, to endure, to sacrifice, and to lose all your terror of the opposition.

Meanwhile, you keep putting one foot in front of the other. You work diligently at your craft. You make up your mind not just to dabble, not to be a dilettante, but to become an expert in your field. You read and you write. A LOT. You make it your mission to keep learning, watching movies new and old, reading scripts, reading books like this one. You analyze and appreciate, you try to determine what's working, what isn't, and why.

You enter the contests, go to pitchfests, you work social media, you work real life, you go to events, to panels, to workshops, and you soak it in, you take notes. You actively seek out ways to keep yourself inspired, you make it a point to bask in works of others that speak to you, and repeat all this as often as necessary. You keep working, you keep writing.

Maybe you get a lowly(ish) assistant job reading scripts and you slog through hundreds, if not thousands, of bad ones. Over time, you start to realize this is probably doing permanent brain damage but, hey, you're learning. You eat a lot of crap. Perhaps you badger friends and family to support you on Kickstarter and make your own short film. You re-read screenwriter Terry Rossio's *Throw in the Towel* **(http://wordplayer.com/columns/wp34.Throw.in.the.Towel.html)** (Google it) for the thousandth time. If you're in L.A., you go to events at the Writers Guild of America or go hang and work at its library and get inspired by and commiserate with other writers. You root for your friends' success, knowing that if they can do this, so can you. You take two steps forward, one step back, you endure. *You keep at it.*

Until perhaps the day comes when you decide you simply don't want to do this anymore, that enough is enough, and that there are plenty of other lovely and meaningful things one can do in the world with this life, and that is perfectly okay, too. In fact, that just may be the smarter way to go.

But in the meantime, you keep at it.

REJECTION, SURVIVAL AND HOW MUCH DO YOU WANT IT?
On dealing with rejection

The short version: it sucks. It's painful and disheartening and immensely aggravating. And it comes with the territory. Boy, oh boy, does it come with the territory. I think the best way to deal with it is to make up your mind to choose to let it fuel you. To let it inspire that little voice inside you that says "Well, I'll show *you*."

In my own work, I have no illusions that I'm creating Art. I'm simply trying, to the best of my ability, to amuse myself and others and to share my own vision. You and I don't have to be everybody's taste and the truth is we never will be. That is simply not the nature of the game, but that's okay.

When I nervously first submitted my finished script for *Only You* to my agent, I had worked on it for almost a year and was barely scraping by. When I called the office, his assistant told me he'd read it and said, "I think you're gonna sell it." I was encouraged, and then he casually added, "People love that crap." Ha. This story is all the more amusing to me in that my agent had told me that this assistant supposedly had something of a crush on me. (Way to a girl's heart.) Regardless, the script did sell in four days for $1 million, up front. As it turned out, he was right, people *did* love that crap. (And in the years since, "people love that crap" has become a catch phrase for my friends and me. You'd be surprised, or maybe you wouldn't, to hear how often it comes in handy.)

I remember waking up the following morning and walking in something of a daze to the local 7-Eleven to buy the trade papers. And there was the announcement of my sale, in black and white, smack dab on the front page of both *The Hollywood Reporter* and *Daily Variety*. I found myself thinking two things: First, "Thank God it wasn't all just a dream." And second, "Well, they're gonna *have* to pay me now. Now that it's been printed in the paper."

Anyway, often when someone rejects or betrays you, lies, cheats, steals, etc., in the business world, there's usually somebody else around to remind you, "It's not personal. It's just business." To which I politely say *bullshit*. Of *course* it's personal. It's always personal when it happens to you, and if you're a creative person, it had *better* be personal. To insist otherwise is patently ridiculous.

However, it's not personal in the larger sense that this is simply the nature of the Hollywood beast. If your goal is to work in this business, you can pretty much bank on the fact that people are going to lie to you and betray you; they're going to steal from you, ignore you, insult you, abuse you, backstab you, and probably much, much more. And yes, they're going to reject you and/or your material. A lot.

In that sense, in the larger aggregate, it isn't personal, as none of us is so special as to be able to escape the inherent ugliness altogether over even a short career, let alone over a long one. Stay in this game long enough and, I don't care who you are, most all of these things are going to happen to you eventually and probably more than once. But—and this is the critical part—if you want it enough, you cannot let that stop you.

You must find a way to let these struggles fuel you. To the best of your ability, you must turn these experiences around on "them" and use them as grist for your own mill. And this is another good time to remind yourself of that fundamental underlying lesson of story: What matters most is not what happens to us, it's what we do about it.

Remember, a hero is one who overcomes great obstacles, right? One who perseveres against all odds. If you want to be a screenwriter, you will have to summon and demonstrate many of the qualities that define a hero, including the willingness to take risks, the courage to keep fighting for what you want, the fortitude, resourcefulness and sheer will to keep going and overcome, outsmart and outlast many an obstacle along the way.

On the flip side, one of the things I like best about Hollywood is that anything can happen. Who'd have thought that John Travolta's career would have been resurrected from the Look Who's Talking doldrums by a former video store movie geek? Who'd have thought that Robert Downey Jr. would go from prison and addiction back to being one of the biggest stars in the world? Life can turn on a dime.

And speaking of Robert Downey Jr., as I mention in my upcoming

Roman Holiday analysis at the end of this chapter, I was briefly rewritten by another writer on my script for *Only You*. (Details about changes that were made to the detriment of my dialogue are available on request.) Anyway, this is a very painful and, sadly, all too common experience for a screenwriter in Hollywood. But, hey, I got paid very well, and I was fortunate enough to be able to go to Italy when it was in production where I met the extraordinary Robert Downey Jr. for the first time. At that moment of introduction, he endeared himself to me forever when he took both my hands in his, leaned very close to me and said, "I just want you to know I loved your script and I never would have changed a word." OMG.

Geraldine Chaplin, actress daughter of Charlie Chaplin, has been quoted as saying regarding Robert's performance in *Chaplin,* "It was as though he had channeled my father." This is coming from the man's own *daughter*. Robert, as pretty much anyone who's been in a movie theater in at least the last twenty or so years knows, is a phenomenon. He somehow seems empathetic almost to the point of being telepathic. He is a kind, generous and incredibly gifted man, and he deserves every bit of the success he has earned.

BONUS: HOW TO WIN A BEST SCREENPLAY OSCAR

I have a theory: if you want a best screenplay Oscar (and who doesn't?), one way to stack the odds in your favor is to write a script about a particularly unlikely, yet not fantastical, event or relationship. If you can find a way to make us buy in and believe, as far-fetched as the story might seem on its surface (and the more far-fetched, yet still human and somehow credible, the better), you're probably onto something.

When you stop to think about it, this makes sense, right? If a story seems very unlikely on its surface, chances are that it's somehow original, and if you're able to manage to convince your audience to suspend disbelief and become invested, then you must be a pretty darn good storyteller. Points for degree of difficulty. Obviously, none of this is the least bit easy, and you have to be able to execute it with excellence, but it is nevertheless worth keeping in mind when brainstorming your next idea if winning an Oscar is on your life's to-do list.

EXAMPLES OF THE UNLIKELY THAT TOOK HOME OSCAR GOLD:

An Unlikely Friendship:
THE KING'S SPEECH (based on a true story)
JUNO
LOST IN TRANSLATION

An Unlikely Winner:
LITTLE MISS SUNSHINE
SLUMDOG MILLIONAIRE (did not win best screenplay but did win best picture)

Two Unlikely Criminals:
THELMA & LOUISE

Another Unlikely Criminal and Even Less Likely Detective:
FARGO

An Unlikely Success Story:
ERIN BROCKOVICH (another true story)
FORREST GUMP
ROCKY
GANDHI (again, true story)

An Unlikely Turn of Events:
THE QUEEN (true story)
Unlikely Coincidences (and, imho, not believable, but that didn't matter to Oscar voters):
CRASH

An Unlikely Twist on History:
SHAKESPEARE IN LOVE

An Unlikely Genius: (written by two unlikely writers)
GOOD WILL HUNTING

An Unlikely Love Affair:
WITNESS
THE CRYING GAME
MOONSTRUCK
THE PIANO

An Unlikely Rescue Mission:
ARGO (yet another true story): This one had the double Oscar-enticing whammy of not only being a stranger-than-fiction true story of courage and suspense, it also made lots of good-natured fun of Hollywood (something else Oscar voters love). And in the end the movie business was the hero, or certainly a hero, of the story. I was convinced this one couldn't miss, and in fact early on that year I placed a bet on it to win the Best Picture Oscar when the conventional money was still on *Lincoln*. I wound up winning $500 (and hope the IRS isn't reading this).

Two Unlikely Film Productions:
THE ARTIST:
Here it's not the story within the film that is particularly unusual or unlikely (it wasn't), but the story behind the film itself. That a silent film in black and white would be made in 2011 and have genuine mass audience appeal was extremely unlikely. I think that's primarily what won the Academy voters over. (For the record, it did not win best screenplay but did receive a nomination for that, and the movie won Best Picture.)

BOYHOOD:

Oscar-wise, the idea that someone would manage to shoot a cohesive film over the course of twelve years seemed extremely unlikely and unusual. But unfortunately for *Boyhood*, I think its hype got a bit ahead of itself, and it wound up the frontrunner a little too early on in the awards season. Thus, the reason I thought it was going to win (its unlikeliness) strangely morphed into the reason it didn't: The unlikely ironically suddenly seemed a little too likely by the time the awards ceremony finally rolled around. The underdog became the odds-on favorite, and Academy voters thus opted for the upset in *Birdman*. (Also, *Birdman* is about show business and, as mentioned above, Hollywood likes movies about that.)

Regardless, what do all these "unlikelies" have in common? Well, first, you'll notice that a number of them are based on true, stranger-than-fiction stories. They're also, of course, all very well-crafted. But equally important, if not even more to the point, regardless of whether they're based on real events or the stuff of fiction, *they're about people defying and transcending our conventional expectations of what is possible.* And part of the almost primal appeal of stories like these is that they remind us of one of the things I like best about Hollywood: Anything can happen.

You may thank me in your speech.

BUSINESS OF SHOWBIZ TAKEAWAYS, PART I:

1. Rejection sucks and is inevitable. It comes with the territory. You must decide to learn what you can from it, ignore the rest and resolutely make up your mind to outlast it.

2. Sometimes what seems to be the worst thing can turn out to be the best. Strive to let your enemies become instruments

of your destiny. Choose to move beyond them, onward and upward, and leave them in the dust.

3. If you want to win an Oscar, you can significantly increase your odds by telling an unlikely but believable story. And if it's a true story about an underdog transcending our conventional beliefs of what is possible, even better.

4. If at all possible, get Robert Downey Jr. to star in your movie.

STRUCTURALLY SPEAKING: ROMAN HOLIDAY

This script is not available online. A hardcopy can, however, be ordered from *scriptfly.com* for $25.

Screenplay by: Ian McLellan Hunter, John Dighton, Dalton Trumbo

Story by: Dalton Trumbo

First, a little bit of history about this movie: It was co-written by John Dighton and Dalton Trumbo. Blacklisted at the time, Trumbo was named a member of the Hollywood Ten and fired for refusing to testify in 1947 before the House Un-American Activities Committee. (*Roman Holiday* was made in 1953, and by then Trumbo was living in Mexico.) Trumbo won three Oscars while blacklisted, including one for this script, for which he was fronted by fellow writer Ian McLellan Hunter. Trumbo died in 1976 and was posthumously awarded the Oscar for the script for *Roman Holiday* in 1993. His writing credit on the film was finally restored in 2003.

Another little bit of trivia, not nearly as significant: I named Robert Downey Jr.'s character, "Damon Bradley," in my movie *Only You* after Gregory Peck's character, "Joe Bradley," in *Roman Holiday*. I related this little personal homage to director Norman Jewison who took it and ran with it, and then tried to cast Marisa Tomei as the new Audrey Hepburn in the public eye. Hence the scene in *Only You* when she and Robert re-enact the Mouth of Truth bit from *Roman Holiday*. For the record, your Honor, I neither wrote nor suggested this scene; I would never have dared. It was written by a writer whom Marisa brought in to replace me, and who, I'm happy to say, received no credit on my movie. So, there's a bit of (old news) gossip for you.

Back to *Roman Holiday* and a little more on the making of the film. Gregory Peck was, of course, a major star at the time. Audrey Hepburn, who wound up winning the best actress Oscar for her performance, was a newcomer and had never had a starring role. But after Peck saw some of the dailies, he thought she was so extraordinary that he insisted she be given equal billing. As you might imagine, this sort of behavior is unheard of in Hollywood. Peck was not only a great actor, he was a true class act of a human being.

And speaking of that, I think this movie is an example of one that really does have two leads. Peck was right to give her equal billing. Each lead has a problem and a goal; each takes action that results in unexpected consequences; each encounters the biggest test of all in Act III, and each has an arc.

ACT I

As the movie opens, we see the Princess' status quo: it's opulent and lavish but also dull and constrictive, especially for a young woman her age. She's forced to entertain stuffy old folks and to go through the motions of regimented behavior ad nauseam. Her problem is that her life is not her own.

Inciting Incident: Later that evening, she hits a breaking point and throws a tantrum; a doctor is called. He gives her a sedative to help her sleep. This is the bolt from the blue and the cause for all that follows. (An aside: There's something just a little bit creepy about that scene, isn't there? The way they sort of hold her down? Even though the doctor does seem sweet and advises her to "do whatever she wants for a little while.")

Shortly thereafter, she takes the good doctor's advice. Outside the palace windows, *la dolce vita* beckons, and she sneaks out into the festive late night streets of Rome. I'd call this Plot Point #1 for her.

And now we cut to the poker game and for the first time meet Peck. Here it's established that he's a newspaperman, low on funds, and has an appointment the following morning to cover the arrival of the princess. As he's walking home, he and the princess "meet cute" when he discovers her sleeping on a public bench, but he doesn't realize who she is. But he's a good guy and thus reluctantly tries to send her home—at his own expense, even—and when that fails, even more reluctantly takes her home with him. This is one of my favorite scenes in the film, when she's still "drunk" and he's both annoyed by and attracted to her. And I love the way they spar over Keats and Shelley.

The next morning after oversleeping and missing his appointment, he rushes to the office, is berated by his boss and for the first time sees her photograph and realizes this is the woman who is now sleeping in his apartment.

Plot Point #1:

For him it's when he realizes who she is and strikes a deal for an exclusive story about her. We learn he's in debt to both his boss and his landlord and that what he most wants, his goal, is a one-way ticket back to New York City. This is the action he takes, and it—she—is going to be his ticket out. His goal is to exploit this opportunity and her for all they're worth.

ACT II

Now the movie takes off in a new direction as she leaves his apartment, and at first Peck surreptitiously follows her, then just "happens" to run into her and manages to convince her to take the day off and spend it with him. There's a travelogue leisureliness to this portion of the movie, one I think you probably couldn't get away with today, but it's one of the things I love about it. I love seeing Rome with them and through their eyes, and I love Eddie Albert's character of the photographer Irving Radovich as well. He's a great foil.

Over the course of this act they have various little adventures, and throughout it they each have the ongoing obstacle of keeping their true identities hidden from each other, (though, of course, we know that he knows hers). So that by the end of the day, when they dance together on the river barge, it's truly moving and I think we really do buy the idea that they become sincerely enamored of each other, especially as she's so sincerely appreciative of his kindness, and we understand he's now starting to feel a bit guilty about what he's been up to all along. But he's not yet ready to give it all up either, which keeps things interesting.

Plot Point #2:

They narrowly manage to escape from the Secret Service agents who show up on the barge to try to take her back "into custody" (battle won), but then soberly realize their time out together is soon going to have to come to an end.

ACT III

There's such a sweet sorrow in these last few scenes of them together again in his apartment. They both encounter their biggest test of all here: In her case, it's whether she's going to do the responsible thing and return to her life and royal duties as a princess, (though honestly, it doesn't seem that she's got much of a choice. Then again, Prince Edward did walk away from the monarchy for Wallis Simpson, didn't he?)

In Peck's case, it's a tougher test, really, in that he does have more of a hard choice to make. But he opts to do the right thing because he's fallen for her. Thus, despite the fact that he realizes they're not going to be together, he chooses to not to reveal her secret and thus will lose his bet with his boss and forgo his chance to move home to New York City.

In terms of character arcs, they're both pretty good people to begin with. She is dutiful and genuinely gracious, and he is a kind enough man that he doesn't leave her sleeping on the street or allow the cab driver to take her to the police. That said, they clearly both grow as a result of their experience together. She seems to grow up, and when she returns to the palace to take up her royal duties, it's with a newfound maturity and sense of self. She's more able to take charge. She passes on the milk and crackers and makes clear to the Countess who is working for whom. And when she stops herself from giving the rote answer to the question of which was her favorite city on the tour and with new-found confidence and self-assurance says, "Rome. By all means, Rome..." that's a pretty great, bittersweet moment.

As for him, obviously he does the right thing. He's ultimately honest with her, reveals himself to be a reporter and gives her the potentially embarrassing photos that his pal had taken without her knowledge. He chooses to give up any money and any notoriety, and thus is going to remain in debt and at the mercy of his boss in Rome.

And that final moment, with him standing there with tears in his eyes before walking out alone, his footsteps echoing in that grand empty hall, in my book is one of the all-time great movie endings.

CHAPTER FOURTEEN

THE BUSINESS OF SHOWBIZ, PART TWO

> *"I realized quickly all I had to do was make people like to read my scripts."*
>
> ~ Brian Duffield, Blacklist winner and produced screenwriter (*Your Bridesmaid is a Bitch, Jane Got a Gun, Insurgent*)

ELL, DUH, RIGHT? WHY DIDN'T we think of that? But obvious as Duffield's advice may seem on its surface, what he's really getting at here is that you want to make the reader's job as easy and enjoyable as possible. That means, among other things: 110 pages or less, no typos or other blatant signs of sloppiness or amateurism. It also means, if at all possible, making friends with the reader via your voice, taking him into your confidence.

NUTS AND BOLTS: PRACTICAL INFORMATION

1. Script Formatting and Submission

In terms of properly formatting your script, if you buy some screenwriting software—Fade In, Final Draft, Movie Magic Screenwriter are currently the most popular—or use the free versions, Celtx or Trelby, lots of steps (including centering a character's name in all caps when he's speaking dialogue, keeping the margins appropriate for action versus dialogue, etc.) will be automatically done for you at the touch of a button. The latest versions will even read your script out loud with different character voices.

Length-wise for a feature screenplay 110 pages is considered standard, but many industry professionals, including writer/ director Lawrence Kasdan, (*Body Heat, The Big Chill, Raiders of the Lost Ark, Star Wars: The Empire Strikes Back, Star Wars: The Force Awakens*, among others) say it's now closer to 100 pages.

In an interesting **podcast (https://itunes.apple.com/us/podcast/ austin-film-festivals-on-story/id580567383)** Kasdan did from the Austin Film Festival in 2011, he insists that *no one* likes to read scripts—no writer, no agent, no producer, no director—including himself. I'm inclined to agree, and certainly nobody likes to read sloppy, bad, overlong scripts, so try not waste anybody's time. Before you ask anyone to read your material, hold it to a high standard and don't give anyone a reason to dismiss you prematurely. The screenwriting software programs will let you cheat the margins and spacing a little bit, but if you do it too much your work will wind up looking cramped and it'll be obvious.

Another formatting guideline, should you decide to go old school and submit a hard copy: put nothing extra on the cover, no artwork, and don't get fancy. You want three-hole paper held together with brass brads and a colored cover. The title, in all caps, should be centered on the title page, with "Written by" and your name below that. That's it.

2. Protect Your Material
Register it with Writers Guild of America.
Writers Guild Script Registry: **www.wgawregistry.org**

You can do this without even without being a member of the Guild for a fee of $20. Highly recommended. And register it with the U.S. Copyright Office: **www.copyright.gov**. The current fee is $35.

The reason I also recommend registering your script with the U.S. Copyright Office in addition to the WGA is that if you ever had to file suit against someone for stealing your material—the sort of thing which, ahem, has been known to happen to the best of us—and you were to actually wind up in court, if you've registered your material with the Feds and you prevail, you're entitled not only to whatever damages you receive but also to your lawyers' fees and court costs. It's worth the extra $35.

You'll also want to keep a detailed log of any script queries or submissions you make and any meetings you engage in regarding it. The log should include the person(s), the company, the place and the date.

BUT PLEASE NOTE: *You cannot copyright an idea.*

This is critical. You can copyright only the *expression* of your idea, not the idea itself. You can copyright the book, the play, the screenplay, etc. Copyright protects "original works of authorship," not the ideas for them.

If you have an idea that you think is all by itself so strong and so high-concept that it's potentially a billion-dollar blockbuster—an idea like, say, *Jurassic Park*—and thus highly steal-able, then don't blab about it, *write it.*

3. Keep It to Yourself

Along the lines of the above, talk, in writing as in life, is cheap. You, like any good protagonist, need to take *action*, to show, not tell. Don't squander your creative energies babbling on about your work to everyone you know. It's fine to run things by a few close, trusted friends and get a sense of whether something is working for people. In fact, that's a good idea. But beyond that, your script should be your little secret. Protect it, nurture it, and don't send it out into the big bad world until it's really, *really* ready.

4. Options

Rarely is a script bought outright for its full purchase price. My deal for *Only You*, with all the money paid up front, was an exception and primarily the result of an aggressive bidding war. If a producer or studio wants to try to produce your work, he or she will typically make an option deal with you.

An option is basically a lease of your material. Say a studio or producer is interested in your work and is hoping to put together a cast, crew and financing to produce it. Rather than buy the script outright and upfront as, alas, there's a good chance that these elements may not all come together, the buyer may offer to take out an option on it, which allows him exclusive rights to shop the project for a limited amount of time for a limited sum. Typically, an option agreement stipulates a number of features, including:

- Option price

- Option term

- The purchase price should the project go forward and be produced

Now, the next part is just my opinion, and reasonable people may disagree, but I would strongly advise you never to option your work for free.

The market for originals these days is tough. *Really* tough. If selling a spec script used to be the equivalent of climbing Everest (which it was), now it's more like mountain climbing on one leg. With no oxygen. The market is simply not what it used to be, dominated as it is by brands, franchises, remakes, reboots, and multi-national conglomerates that don't want to spend $50 million to make $150 million, which, to my way of thinking, still seems like pretty good money. Nope, instead major buyers would prefer to spend $300 million in hopes of making $1 billion. And with that kind of money on the line, the safer bet is almost always on an established brand. Going with a known brand also allows executives to far more easily cover their asses if the movie flops than if they'd really stuck their necks out to support an original.

So it can be quite tempting when someone—anyone—comes along and flatters you and tells you he likes your work and would like to try to set it up. He just needs a little time. That's great, but he needs to *pay you something* for that time and that privilege. Think how much time and effort you have invested in what you've written. If you treat your work as though it's worth nothing, why should others see it any differently? What does it say about the value that you place on your time, your labor, and what you've created if you're willing to simply give it away? It's a simple fact of human nature that people do not typically value what they get for nothing.

Legitimate producers who are genuinely in a position to get your work seen and read by people who are in a position to finance it have the money to option it *if* they truly deem it worthy. The wannabes and posers don't. You are, of course, free to disagree, to find exceptions and rationalize and give your work away. It's just my humble opinion: Never option your work for nothing, and whatever you decide to do, get it in writing.

5. Getting Covered

"Coverage" is the term for what agencies and studios use to evaluate your material. It's effectively the book report a reader creates about your script for higher-ups who generally prefer to read as little as humanly possible. The layout of these forms varies a bit from company to company, but it's a safe bet that the criteria listed below are generally the ones upon which your script will be evaluated. Coverage includes a reader's summary of your log line, though you or your agent or manager will probably provide that in the cover email; a one-to-two-page synopsis; and a critique.

There's also typically a chart that rates the following:

- Premise

- Characters

- Story Line (or Plot)

- Dialogue

- Production Values

- Structure is usually in there, too, but can be contained in Story Line

- Budget Estimate

Finally, the script will be rated overall. The three ratings are usually Pass, Consider and Recommend.

> *"I liked the old studio system with the powerful moguls better. At least in those days you knew whose ass to kiss."*
>
> ~ Billy Wilder

6. Agents, Managers and Lawyers: Be prepared to pay, but only if it sells

Never—and I mean *never*—pay any money up front to an agent or manager. This one is not debatable. Agents should work only on commission and take a standard 10%. And by the way, agents do not find you work. They, as an irritated Sydney Pollack maintains in *Tootsie*, "field offers." Having said that, it's tough to get an offer without one, unless you are somehow personally particularly well-connected. And in my experience they do less and less. Agents are primarily in the "branding" business now, and they're typically not interested in you unless you've already sold yourself first, meaning that you have a huge web following, have won a noted contest, created your own indie film, etc.

Managers take 10% to 15% but ostensibly hold your hand more and are more willing to take on an unknown. You don't *have* to have a manager, but it has become pretty much the industry standard as agents do less all the time in terms of career building and guidance. Agents basically negotiate the deal, once you and your manager have managed to interest somebody in making one.

Lawyers take 5% and most work only on commission, not hourly, which means that in order to return your phone calls, they have to think there's money in it for them.

Then the Writers Guild of America takes 1½%. If you add it all up, that's a whopping 31.5% off the top. Suddenly that million-dollar deal is no longer a million dollars, and that's before taxes.

7. Breaking and Entering: Contests, Labs, Pitchfests and other methods of getting you and your work seen, represented and sold

Often the first question I get from aspiring writers, even writers who have yet to complete their first screenplay is, "How do I get an agent?" Okay, first, until you've finished a script (or more like three or four) you don't need an agent and an agent definitely doesn't need you.

Second, I consider agents a necessary evil. And both those words are applicable: "necessary" and "evil." Oh, *okaaaaay*, some of them aren't really evil. They just act that way. Regardless, they have a job to do, and being your friend isn't part of it—*until* and unless you represent real money to them. In order for you to do that, you have to either land your own gig, develop your own following, (generally online, via a blog, graphic novel, fan fiction, etc.), create your own film, or at least catch their eye via some means other than begging for their attention.

Following are a few of the more legitimate and accepted ways to do this:

CONTESTS:

Below is a list of what are currently considered the most well-respected and well-known contests. Winning a contest, or even placing in the semi-finals, depending on the contest, is one of the best ways there is to get your work seen by those who can help sell it and you. The top contest winners are taken seriously by the people whose job it is to find and represent new writers. There seem to be new contests and fellowships springing up all the time, so be sure to do your due diligence before sending off a registration fee.

For further details regarding each of these, including website links, current entry requirements and deadlines, please visit my website at **dianedrake.com.** A calendar of current events and deadlines can be found under the Blog tab and also on my Contact page.

1. Academy Nicholl Fellowships in Screenwriting

The biggest, most well-respected and highest paying contest out there is the Nicholl Fellowships in Screenwriting Competition, put on every year by the Academy of Motion Picture Arts and Sciences.

I've heard that the contest assigns roughly 250 scripts to each reader. That's a veritable boatload of reading and in many cases, if not most, it's a chore. Remember it's the readers you first have to impress, so try not to make their job any more difficult than it already is. Submit only your best, most polished work. Doing so will endear you to them and help enable you to stand out in the crowd.

The Academy Nicholl Fellowships in Screenwriting competition awards up to five $35,000 fellowships to amateur screenwriters. Fellowship winners are invited to participate in awards week ceremonies and seminars and are expected to complete at least one original feature film screenplay during the fellowship year.

Although the competition claims to entertain all genres equally, in my experience and from what I've read, Nicholls tends to have a bit of a bias for drama.

2. The Big Break Contest
This contest for television and film scripts is sponsored by the creators of the Final Draft software. "Eleven winners share cash, prizes and the New York Film Academy Writing Fellowship" with a total value over $80,000," the website says. The contest has seven main genre categories for feature entries.

3. Austin Film Festival, "The Writers Festival"
This festival is for films, screenplays and teleplays. In the feature screenplay competition, there are two first prizes, one for drama, one for comedy, each of which includes a $5,000 cash award, plus airfare and hotel for the festival. This is a very popular and fun festival that focuses especially on writers and is held every autumn in Austin, Texas. Highly recommended.

4. PAGE Awards
The PAGE International Screenwriting Awards competition was established in the fall of 2003 by an alliance of Hollywood producers, agents, and development executives. Their goal: "to discover the most exciting new scripts by up-and-coming writers from across the country and around the world."

5. Fresh Voices Screenplay Competition
Fresh Voices promises $15,000 in cash and prizes, free feedback and "guaranteed consideration from leading Hollywood Production companies."

6. Scriptapalooza Screenplay Competition
Scriptapalooza says it will promote, pitch and push all semifinalists for one year, giving the writers opportunities to sign agents or

managers and have their scripts optioned or made into movies. Over $50,000 in prizes is awarded, and screenwriters can order feedback with their submissions.

7. Slamdance Screenplay Competition
Slamdance features four categories: Feature, Short, Horror and Original Teleplay, and awards the top three screenplays in each category.

8. American Zoetrope Screenplay Contest
Created by Francis Ford Coppola, the contest says the winner and ten finalists will be considered for representation by various agencies, including William Morris and CAA, and their scripts will be considered for film option and development by leading production companies. Professional readers read the scripts, and Coppola selects the winner.

9. BlueCat Screenplay Contest
Put on by Gordy Hoffman and his team, this competition features a $15,000 grand prize and four $2,500 prizes for the finalists. It also has special separate entry categories for best short screenplay, best screenplay from the United Kingdom, best screenplay from India, and a category for entries from outside the US, Canada or the UK.

10. The Tracking Board Contest - Launchpad
These are contests for TV pilots and feature films. Sponsors say they are looking for marketability, high concept, and high salability.

11. ScriptPipeline Competitions
The organization sponsors a variety of contests for screenwriting, TV writing, students and even "great ideas" with varying deadlines. It offers $25,000 to the winning script and says that with this come introductions to managers, producers, agents, etc.

12. WeScreenplay
WeScreenplay offers $10,000 in prizes, announcements of winners in InkTip Magazine and MovieBytes, as well as script distribution to producers, agents and managers.

LABS, FELLOWSHIPS and MENTORSHIPS:

1. Sundance Screenwriters Lab
Sundance is probably the most well-known, well-respected and oldest program of its kind. The emphasis here is on indie, lower budget, non-studio types of projects. Some successful recent films to have gone through the Sundance Lab include *Beasts of the Southern Wild*, *The Lunchbox*, and *Whiplash*.

From the website: "The Screenwriters Lab is a five-day writers' workshop that gives independent screenwriters the opportunity to work intensively on their feature film scripts with the support of established writers in an environment that encourages innovation and creative risk-taking. Through one-on-one story sessions with Creative Advisors, Fellows engage in an artistically rigorous process that offers them indispensable lessons in craft, as well as the means to do the deep exploration needed to fully realize their material."

2. New York Women in Film and Television Writers Lab
The Writers Lab brings eight women screenwriters over the age of forty together with established mentors from the film industry for an intimate gathering and intensive workshop at Wiawaka Center for Women on Lake George, N.Y.

The only program of its kind, the Writers Lab evolved in recognition of the absence of the female voice in narrative film, along with the dearth of support for script development. The lab offers eight promising films by women over forty a springboard to production.

3. International Screenwriters Association Fast Track Fellowship

Two winners are flown to LA for five days to be mentored by agents and producers. Both are featured on the association's success stories page. They say that the ISA team will spend a year working with both writers through the association's development program.

4. ScreenCraft

Contests and mentorships are divided into genres and forms, with various deadlines and rewards.

PITCHFESTS:

These gatherings are an opportunity to put yourself and your work in front of agents, managers, producers and other executives. Pitchfests have become popular and represent one more way for newcomers to try to bring their work to the attention of those with the money, connections and means to produce it.

Writer participants typically have five minutes in which to impress the executives enough that they want to read your material and/or follow up further. Basically it's speed-dating for writers/producers/managers/agents. You'll want to keep your pitch very short, just one or two minutes, so that you have a little bit of time to just converse with the person, introduce yourself, respond to follow-up questions, etc.

I suppose pitchfests are like a lot of things in life, you pay your money and you take your chances. There will always be people for whom the experience goes well and who therefore think the process is well worth it. And I imagine there are others for whom it doesn't go so well and they are not as enthusiastic. Regardless, there are also usually classes and consultations and, of course, the opportunity to meet other writers, which is valuable in itself. But the main event is, obviously, the pitching.

If you decide to attend, be sure to do your homework before you go. Research the companies you'll be pitching. You don't want to pitch a horror project to a company that specializes in family films or vice-versa. Passes come at various prices and offer various amounts of access.

Oh, and before you go, you might also want to take a look at this wickedly funny short film. It's a painfully, blackly hilarious and inspired satire of the process and the nature of Hollywood.

Recommended WATCH: DEAD IN THE ROOM Written by Marjory Kaptanoglu; Directed by Adam Pertofsky
(https://vimeo.com/19053229)

1. Great American Pitchfest
Held at the end of May in Burbank, CA,the pitchfest is a one-day event and is as part of the larger three-day event called Scriptfest.

The founders of this event claim to enable you to pitch your script to more than 120 production companies, agents, managers, financiers, and other industry professionals seeking material to option, and writers to hire, manage, and represent. Only 500 tickets are sold, and it is said to sell out every year.

2. The Hollywood Pitch Festival
This festival has a lengthy and impressive list of companies and agencies attending. The focus of this two-and-a-half-day event seems to be largely on the pitching, with comparatively few speakers or workshops, as more time appears to be devoted to actual pitch meetings and opportunities.

3. Story Expo
Held in September near Los Angeles International Airport, Story Expo bills itself as "the world's biggest convention of writers from all mediums: screenwriters, TV writers, novelists, filmmakers, gamers, journalists, graphic novelists, actors, business people, comic book writers and more." The event is said to feature over

110 world-renowned speakers, more than 100 classes and 30-plus exhibitors. Story Expo sponsors say it covers all aspects of story and writing, from craft to business to pitching to career.

NEW MEDIA

A fairly new and welcome wrinkle in this game is the entry of Amazon Studios into the television and film production market. Not only are they a valuable source of production money, in contrast to most every other major producer out there, they've opted to engage in what they call an "open-door policy," and are encouraging the submission of unsolicited material. They're currently accepting scripts and concept videos for film, and drama, comedy and children's television series. Obviously, one assumes they're receiving a vast multitude of submissions, but what the heck? I think this one is worth looking into, especially for those without representation.

https://studios.amazon.com/submit/film

https://studios.amazon.com/submit/series/comedy

https://studios.amazon.com/submit/series/drama

SCREENPLAY EXPOSURE SERVICES

1. The Black List: *www.blcklst.com*
The Black List grew out of a private survey that a smart guy named Franklin Leonard, who at the time was working as an executive in development for Leonardo DiCaprio, created at the end of each year starting in 2005. He asked a select list of agents and producers to name their favorite un-produced scripts of the year, then tabulated the data and published the list. Many of these scripts went on to be produced, and the Black List has become a recognized identifier of good material.

In October 2012, Leonard introduced a new business model that endeavors to allow lesser known and unrepresented writers get their work seen as well. A separate Black List is now open to all writers wanting professional exposure, evaluation and feedback. For a fee, writers can upload their scripts to the Black List database, have their work evaluated and, if the evaluation is good, opt to share it with what the company claims are more than 1,000 film industry professionals. If the evaluation is not so good, writers can choose to forgo that sharing part of the process.

I admire what Leonard has done in the past and has tried to create here. I think I'll be more of a believer when I start seeing more movies being made from the scripts writers themselves have submitted and not just from the pool of already represented and produced working writers who make the original Black List that Leonard still publishes every year. Regardless, it's another good option to keep in mind.

2. InkTip: *www.inktip.com*
This is a log line and script listing service similar to Black List. Ink Tip claims a network of over 4,000 Industry professionals. You can view current rates, success stories and more on its site.

OTHER USEFUL BUSINESS-RELATED WEBSITES:
Obviously, these are always changing; the following are a few stalwarts:

1. The Writers Guild of America: *www.wga.org*
The WGA hosts numerous events a year, many of which are open to the public. The Writers Guild Foundation, *www.wgfoundation. org,* which is a separate entity, also puts on its own events. Both are highly recommended. And for those who don't live in Los Angeles, sometimes they stream live events on Ustream, so check into that.

George Clooney, Alexander Payne, Katherine Bigelow, Mark Boal, Ben Affleck, Judd Apatow, Florian Henckel Von Donnersmarck, Charlie Kaufman, Steve Levitan, Nia Vardalos, Owen Wilson—

these are just a few of the gifted people I've enjoyed hearing speak in person about the art and craft of movie-making and story-telling. If you're in L.A. and are serious about becoming a screenwriter, there is simply no good excuse for not availing yourself of these learning opportunities.

When I saw Von Donnersmarck, the brilliant writer/director of *The Lives of Others,* I was so impressed by his intelligence and graciousness that I thought, "I wanna be your friend. I wanna come to your family barbeques and talk about big ideas and art and meaning and life." I, of course, said none of this to him (which is undoubtedly just as well). But I would advise you not to be like me, don't be shy. Speak up, say hello, let the people you've heard speak know how much you appreciated them and the insight and knowledge they've shared. Just don't be a weirdo.

2. Scriptwriters Network: *www.scriptwritersnetwork.com*
This organization hosts speaker panels, runs a High Concept Screenplay competition, offers a variety of events and services, and cohosts a monthly networking event in Los Angeles called Friday Night Social, originally created by a good friend of mine, story consultant and author Jen Grisanti. If you go, say hi to Jen.

3. Tracking Board: *tracking-board.com*
This paid membership site, ($79 per year) contains industry information and tracks the spec market, including what and who is hot in the screenwriting world. It also tracks which spec scripts are going out around town and which have sold and offers a feature and pilot competition.

4. Deadline Hollywood: *www.deadline.com*
This is one of the only sites that gives you the straight scoop about the deal-making/business side of what's going on in the entertainment world, from both the reporters and the savvy commenters, and not just some publicist's b.s.

5. Hollywood Stock Exchange: *www.hsx.com*
This site provides an up-to-the minute snapshot of who's hot and who's not among players, projects, releases and companies.

6. Stage 32: *www.stage32*
This site claims to be the premier social network for film, television and theater creatives and is free to join.

7. Talentville: *www.talentville.com*
Started by Ben Cahan, this is an online community for writers with lots of helpful information, message boards, opportunities for networking, feedback and a monthly contest.

8. ISA: International Screenwriters Association: *www.networkisa.org*
With an international membership of over 80,000, the ISA is a supportive networking group that provides writers with extensive informational resources for career development in screenwriting. They also provide a forum for film and TV producers to seek and discover new talent.

OTHER ANGLES:

1. Query Letters
This is obviously the old-school way to go. I'm not a huge fan, as I think the time and effort expended are generally disproportionate to the chances of success, especially when it comes to approaching producers. For smaller boutique managers and even agents, however, I think this is still a potentially viable way to go. Just as there are reportedly many roads to God and production, this is one more to keep in mind if the situation seems appropriate. Just make sure your letter is short, polite, to the point and, ideally, at least mildly entertaining. This is a case of first impressions, and you want to make sure yours is a good one or there is no point in bothering.

2. Social Media

The more current and recommended way to get an agent or producer is to build your own following and make the suits come to you. But nobody said this was easy. Obviously everyone knows all about Facebook and the rest, and how tired some of us are of others who are forever promoting themselves and their projects and begging for "likes." So if you're going to use social media please strive to be clever about it, not just annoyingly persistent.

And speaking of cleverness, here's an angle to consider: Tweet as one of your characters.

> *"Nothing is real and you are cosmically insignificant, so relax."*
>
> ~ God

The former head writer for *The Daily Show*, David Javerbaum, created the hilarious account "Tweets of God," in which he tweets as The Creator. The above quote is one of my favorite examples of His work. God's twitter following, which currently stands at over 2 million, led Javerbaum to write a Broadway play called *An Act of God*, currently running in Los Angeles and starring Sean Hayes.

3. DIY

Sometimes you just have to take matters into your own hands and do things in actual real life. Here are a couple of the best, seizing-the-reins DIY examples I've heard:

While still in college, Mindy Kaling, now famous from *The Office* and *The Mindy Project* as well as two books, and her then-writing partner, Brenda Withers, wrote a hilarious little play called *Matt & Ben*, about how the screenplay for *Good Will Hunting* literally fell from the ceiling one day into the modest apartment Matt Damon and Ben Affleck were sharing in college.

Just this premise amuses me immensely, capitalizing as it did on the rumors that swirled around that script and its origins in Hollywood at the time, especially after Damon and Affleck won the best screenplay Oscar for it. (One rumor was that William Goldman was really the brains of the operation. Goldman has vehemently denied this.)

Regardless, not only did these two very clever women come up with this idea and execute it exceedingly well, they wrote it for themselves to star in—while still in college(!) How ballsy and inventive is that? They managed to get it up on stage, where it was discovered by Greg Daniels, the then-new show runner of the American version of *The Office*, and the rest is history (certainly at least for Kaling).

Finally, I love the story Mark Boal, who wrote and won the best screenplay Oscar for *The Hurt Locker,* once told at the Writers Guild about getting his movie seen.

After having overcome the major hurdles of finding the financing and shooting the film, the creators were still struggling to find a distributor. They managed to get the movie booked into two small theaters in New York City, hoping to qualify for an Oscar nomination. On its opening weekend, Boal stood on a street corner with his teenage nephew and handed out free tickets to passersby with the hope that if they could just fill the house, perhaps the theater owners would book the film for another week. Again, the rest is history. And that, my friends, is determination and dedication to one's craft.

I cherish stories like these because they inspire us, they help keep us going. And they remind us how important it is to take action and just get out there and do something to make our dreams a reality.

It's a very challenging time to be a screenwriter. In recent years, franchises, superheroes, and brands have overtaken original stories, and many studios have consolidated. But still, there are those amazing exceptions to the rules that manage to somehow slip through the cracks every year, get made and show up on the screen. They are a testament to perseverance and resourcefulness, and are examples to look up to.

BUSINESS OF SHOWBIZ TAKEAWAYS, PART II:

1. Brevity is the soul of wit and screenplays. Keep your feature script under 110 pages or risk incurring the wrath of readers everywhere.

2. You should register your work with both the Writers Guild of America and the U.S. Copyright Office.

3. Coverage is the report written by a reader and is what an agent, manager, producer or studio will use to evaluate your work.

4. There are more options and venues to get your work seen than ever before: contests, pitchfests, labs, mentorships, online sites, etc. Do your homework and due diligence on the ones that interest you, then selectively take advantage of these many opportunities. Visit my website, **www. dianedrake.com**, for more details and deadlines.

5. Other ideas for getting your work seen include: make your own short, create your own graphic novel, tweet as your lead, and write the good old-fashioned query letter.

6. Never option your work for free. People do not value what they get for nothing. And never pay an agent or manager up front for representation.

7. If you're in Los Angeles, go to events offered by the Writers Guild of America and Writers Guild Foundation. If you're not, take advantage of their offerings online, and find or create your own writers' group wherever you are.

STRUCTURALLY SPEAKING: SIDEWAYS

READ: SIDEWAYS Screenplay
(http://scriptpipeline.com/wp-content/uploads/2014/08/
Sideways.pdf)

Screenplay by: Alexander Payne & Jim Taylor

Based on the novel by: Rex Pickett

For all its commercial success and critical acclaim, this is fundamentally an indie film. It was released by Fox Searchlight, which is the branch of the company that distributes independent film; it's not what one would call high concept; and it doesn't feature bankable stars. Consequently, because of its low budget (it supposedly cost just $16 million and made over $100 million) and the expectation that it's aimed at more of a niche audience, there's some leeway in terms of structure. It's a little bit looser, more leisurely paced, and more of a character study—a dysfunctional character study—than a plot-driven piece. It's a thoughtful movie for grown-ups. That said, it has plenty of conflict, suspense, humor, even action. It's structurally solid and its heroes do have clear goals, which we become caught up in wondering whether or not they'll accomplish.

Also, it's interesting to me that both lead characters—both "heroes"— are, basically, idiots. Okay, maybe not idiots, but definitely significantly flawed. Alexander Payne, the director who co-wrote the script with Jim Taylor, based on a novel by Rex Pickett, does not offer an airbrushed view of life. His thing is warts and all, with maybe a greater emphasis on the warts.

I had the pleasure of meeting Payne at a Writers Guild screening of the film and asked him if he'd had any qualms about having his characters be such, for lack of better word, dopes. I especially wondered about the scene in Act I in which Miles steals the money from his mother. I thought that was a pretty bold move and wondered if he ever was concerned that that might make an audience stop caring what happened to Miles, that it might make him seem just too unsympathetic. (As a friend who saw the movie said it had done for her.) In response, Payne leaned in and very seriously said, "We're trying to be *real*."

Still, Payne's world view is not as cynical and nihilistic as that of, say, the Coen brothers'. For all his cynicism and unblinkered view of human nature, he definitely does offer glimpses of sheer pleasure and joy, as, for example, in the scene in which they all have a picnic in the vineyard at sunset, and he also ultimately leaves the audience with a feeling of hope.

And, although both characters are kind of idiots, we still care about what happens to them. (Or at least I did, though it's funny to read a few of the more negative reviews on Amazon and see how many people, like my friend, didn't.)

Anyway, assuming that you agree with me, how does that happen? As I've said, it's important to make sure your audience cares about what happens to your hero(es), because if they don't, then why should they bother to stick with the movie? I think one reason we care about Miles is that he's suffered. He has been treated unfairly by the fates. He truly loves his art, he has worked very hard for a long time, is sincere, dedicated and genuinely talented, but there is no room in the commercial world for his work. It appears to have all been for naught.

In addition, his ex-wife left him (one assumes not without reason) and has moved on well while he is still alone. But in terms of his flaws, which are many, he has also been complicit in his own misery. He's basically an alcoholic, often morose, wallowing too much in self-pity and in the past rather than appreciating what's right in front of him. And he has bought into the idea that the commercial world's judgment on his work is the one that matters most. Meanwhile, Jack is just hilariously selfish, coasting on his unctuous, boyish charm and what remains of his fading celebrity and fading good looks. But he's fun and funny, and he's full of enthusiasm and life.

All of that having been said, I think the primary redeeming quality of both of these clowns, the main reason we care about what happens to them, is that they seem to genuinely care about and support each other (even if they often don't seem to really like each other very much). In that, they are good guys. To paraphrase Blake Snyder, it's "Save the Idiot."

Miles plans this trip for Jack and, you could reasonably argue, ultimately risks his life for him when he goes back to retrieve Jack's wedding rings. And Jack is forever sincerely encouraging Miles, both professionally and romantically. Even if Jack is naive, (clueless is more like it), he's a true believer in his friend. The buddies are opposites: Miles neurotic and morose, Jack hedonistic and reckless. They balance each other, there's that orchestration of characters. They're both sort of boneheads, but each in his own individual way.

ACT I

In the opening minutes of the film, not a lot happens. In fact, what does happen seems rather ordinary and pedestrian, but if you look closely, you can see we're being told quite a bit about Miles and his status quo. First, he's hungover; he's been rudely awakened because he parked badly the night before (as a result of driving drunk, one assumes); his car and apartment are modest and worn; and he's a sucker for a good book. He gets caught up in reading as he sits on the toilet, despite the fact that he's already running late.

We also meet Jack, who's killing time with his wealthy in-laws-to-be and his fiancee, and eager to get out of there as soon as possible.

Inciting Incident: When Miles picks Jack up and they take off on the trip, that's the change in the status quo, the cause for all that follows. It isn't, however, as most often is the case with the Inciting Incident, so much something that happens *to* them; it's something they choose.

Plot Point #1:

33 minutes in: Jack, who has already told us that his goal is to get both of them laid, hits on wine-pourer Stephanie and arranges a dinner date that evening with her and Miles' crush, Maya, for the two of them. It's the action he takes to achieve his goal (and his goal for Miles).

Miles' stated external goal is simpler: to play some golf, drink some wine, enjoy the week. There's not really much of a movie in that. His other goal is to sell his book, but for now that is out of his hands; it's not something he's taking action toward as this story progresses. Meanwhile, what Miles *needs* is to get over his ex-wife, stop feeling so sorry for himself, probably to stop drinking so much and be brave enough to try to find love again.

ACT II

All sorts of unexpected complications result for both of them in Act II. Miles really does seem to fall in love, I think he always was quite smitten with Maya; and Jack sweeps Stephanie off her feet and starts to believe he's in love as well, though we know that "in lust" would probably be a more accurate description. Regardless, she buys it.

Throughout Act II the story repeatedly raises hope, then dashes it, then raises it, then dashes it, especially for Miles with respect to Maya. Hills and valleys, twists and turns ensue. (This movie really ought to be called *Ups & Downs*, not *Sideways*.) The lovely scene of subtext between Miles and Maya when they're drawn together discussing Pinot Noir is interestingly actually almost exactly at the **Midpoint** of the film. It's a both a big up, where she seems genuinely romantically interested in him, where it looks like he has a shot, and then a big letdown when he blows the moment.

Despite his faux pas, Miles finally does manage to win Maya over and winds up spending the night with her, but then shortly thereafter he slips up and inadvertently admits that Jack is about to get married, thus revealing that the two of them have effectively been lying to her and Stephanie all along. As a result, Maya is understandably furious and cuts him off completely.

Incidentally, we don't actually see Miles tell her the truth in this scene. We cut from his look of recognition that he's accidentally spilled the beans when he mentions the rehearsal dinner straight to her being outraged. Okay, first, great cause and effect here. Second, there's no need to repeat expositional information, so Payne wisely skips past all that the audience already knows and cuts straight from Miles' "oops" expression to the middle of Maya's justifiably indignant reaction.

Plot Point #2:

The lowest point for Miles, I think, is the one-two punch of losing Maya and then finding out his book hasn't sold because the publisher can't figure out how to market it and his agent is giving up. From here he completely nosedives, gets into that fight at the winery and, in a moment of excruciating self-destruction, pours the contents of the tasting bucket all over himself.

As for Jack, shortly thereafter Stephanie shows up, wallops him and breaks his nose, and he and his buddy wind up in the emergency room.

ACT III

Miles rises from the ashes and turns a bit of a corner when he—not incidentally stone cold sober—calls Maya from the hospital and takes responsibility. He again apologizes, tells her what the time with her has meant to him, and comes clean when he tells her the truth that his book is not really being published and confesses he's "not really a writer." (This is untrue, by the way; Miles *is* a writer for having written, but I digress.)

From here, Miles, Jack and their friendship are all tested further. Finally, I can't let Act III go without mentioning that hilarious little beat when, in the Buffalo restaurant, after Jack tells their enamored waitress, Cammie, that he's a soap actor, an irritated Miles excuses himself to go to the bathroom, and Payne lets the camera linger for a few extra beats on the door and the word MEN. Ha.

One could argue that Jack hits his true nadir after he's forced to run home naked and then realizes he's left his wallet with the wedding rings in it at the waitress' house. Regardless, Miles steps up here and goes to his rescue, and it's a pretty heart-stopping sequence and hilarious Act III battle between him and her lunatic husband.

Finally, this film has a lovely ending and final resolution. Payne shows such a delicate touch here, with that image of Miles driving in the rain as we hear Maya's voice message play over it. And everything is not completely wrapped up neatly with a bow; it's just a graceful, generous bit of hope that we're left with as Miles knocks on her door.

Character Arcs: In terms of who is the main character, if I had to pick one, I'd say it's Miles. This is very much a buddy movie; it's pretty evenly divided, both men get plenty of screen time and have their own problems and goals, but we start and we end with Miles, and we arguably care more about his fate.

Does Jack have an arc? I would emphatically say no. He may tearfully admit that he "knows he's a bad person," but that doesn't make him a changed person. At the end he seems exactly the same shallow, charming, philandering knucklehead he was when the story began; he's not really grown or changed or evolved at all, and despite his getting married, I predict he'll be cheating on his new wife in a matter of weeks, if not days.

Miles, on the other hand, does seem to grow. First, he steps up in the end and takes some bold action. He's heroic in an admittedly completely absurd way when he risks his life to get Jack's wedding rings back. Second, he's honest with Maya about his book. Third, he does suck it up and attend Jack's wedding, where he's gracious to his ex-wife and her new husband, he doesn't drink too much or have a meltdown there. And most important, in the end he's brave enough to go after the girl.

CHAPTER FIFTEEN

ON BEING A "CONTENT CREATOR"

> *"I am always doing that which I cannot do, in order that I may learn how to do it."*
>
> ~ Pablo Picasso

ABOUT HALFWAY THROUGH THE SCREENWRITING class I teach for UCLA, I usually make an announcement to my students. I tell them I've realized there's something very important about screenwriting that I had somehow previously neglected to mention: It's *hard*.

I don't think there's anyone who has sat down to write a screenplay for the first (or the hundredth) time who hasn't come face to face with this painful reality at some point. It's at moments like these that's it's important to remember why you wanted to do this in the first place. I've talked a lot about craft and mechanics and the realities of the marketplace. Now I'd like to come full circle, back to the point of it all.

What is equally if not more important than wisely structuring your story is that you allow your emotion onto the page. You wanted to write this script for a reason, you had something to say, and you want to allow your own voice and personality to speak up and be heard. Write what is in your heart.

Here are a few more things to keep in mind:

DON'T WAIT FOR PERMISSION

Don't wait for someone to wave a wand and make you a Writer.

If you write, you *are* a writer. Own it by doing it. By the same token, if you don't write, if all you do is talk about it, then you're not a writer, you're a talker. Remember Gandhi's words, "Action expresses priorities."

After I'd left Sydney's company and before I managed to land the treatment writing assignment with Hanna-Barbera, I went to a friend's wedding feeling very unemployed and very low. There I ran into another writer named Gary Goldstein, whom I didn't (and don't) really know. But as one does at such social gatherings he asked what I was doing, and I literally could barely mumble the words that I was "trying to write." I was truly so pathetic, it's a wonder he didn't try to put me out of my misery right then and there. But instead, his response was the perfect one: "That's wonderful!" he said with enthusiasm. "It's a great racket." That encouragement, that devil-may-care ease of his phrasing, heartened me. Sure, it wasn't the hardest thing in the world to achieve, and I wasn't pitiful or foolish for trying and thinking maybe I could be a writer—it was "a great racket."

EMBRACE THE PROCESS

When I was in elementary school, we had this extra-curricular activity that went by a rather ridiculously grand name, (especially given that this was in Van Nuys, California), of "Yacht Club." Contrary to the visions this might conjure of eight-year-olds sipping martinis harborside, Yacht Club was an opportunity to build your own toy boat, which was pretty cool.

You began by gluing two wooden 2x4s together vertically, to form a tall rectangle. Next, came the planing; you'd shave down the rectangle into something more boat hull-like. Then you'd begin filing, shaping it further. After that came the rough sandpaper, gradually replaced by finer and finer textures, until the wood felt like silk under your fingertips. Once all this was finished, *then* you got to varnish it. You worked the entire boat at every stage. You didn't jump to polishing one section while you were still planing another.

If it's not already painfully obvious, this is an analogy for a screenplay. Just get that rough draft—warts, rough edges and all—down, and don't start rewriting until you have. That way lies madness. *Trust me on this.*

There's a probably apocryphal story about how Michelangelo created his David by simply cutting away all the excess marble and revealing the extraordinary sculpture residing within. Would that such a thing were possible! Would that we could go straight to the story in its most perfect form and not spend so much time stumbling and fumbling around and going down dead ends.

I have found myself lamenting this law of writing physics many a time. After going down my umpteenth blind alley only to suddenly discover that the solution to some story problem was lying right there by the side of the road all along, I'd think, why couldn't I just have gone straight there? Why didn't I see that right off the bat? It's like a riddle, the answer seems so easy and obvious once you've figured it out. And you think, damn, if only I'd come up with that days (or sometimes weeks) earlier, I would have saved myself so much time and effort and grief.

But, generally speaking, that's simply not the way the creative process works. Even Leonardo da Vinci roughed things out, erased, changed, recalibrated. And I bet even Michelangelo worked in stages. Sometimes the stars align in your favor and you get that flash of lightning inspiration that comes fully formed, but more often than not, writing is a process, in the same way that molding clay, or layering paint on canvas or learning to cook is a process. And if you show up often enough, and put in enough effort, that consistency yields results. Many have observed that the Muses like to see you putting in your time before they'll deign to get off their serene asses and lend you a helping hand.

On a related note, years ago I saw writer/director Richard LaGravanese speak. When asked about writers block, he said,

"Writer's block is when you think you're doing it alone." Which I took to mean it's when your ego gets in the way of the collective unconscious, the energy and mystery of the imagination that is always "out there" for all of us to tap into.

At some point in the writing process you may come up against some of the same fears and difficulties and stumbling blocks that most writers do. And when you do, if you do, I think it's helpful to remember that this, really, is the goal: to tell your truth and to allow the collective unconscious, what Elizabeth Gilbert calls your "creative genius," to assist you.

Writing is about perseverance and tenacity as much as anything. Very few of us are prodigies, and even prodigies screw up from time to time. But all of us can choose to be tenacious. We can choose to keep learning and working hard and thus to keep progressing.

DON'T BE TOO HARD ON YOURSELF, OR YOUR MATERIAL, AND ESPECIALLY NOT AT FIRST

Here's the thing: You may be new to this, and your ideas are probably (mostly anyway) new as well. Ed Catmull, the head of Pixar and Walt Disney Animation in his book, *Creativity Inc.: Overcoming the Unseen Forces That Stand in the Way of True Inspiration*, repeatedly makes the point that you have to allow your creative work, particularly in the early stages, to be what he calls "the ugly baby." As he puts it:

> *"The Ugly Baby idea is not easy to accept. Having seen and enjoyed Pixar movies, many people assume that they popped into the world already striking, resonant and meaningful—fully grown, if you will. In fact, getting them to that point involved months, if not years, of work. If you sat down and watched any early reels of any of our films, the ugliness would be painfully clear. Our job is to protect our*

babies from being judged too quickly. Our job is to protect the new."

Later he adds:

"Many of us have a romantic idea about how creativity happens: A lone visionary conceives of a film or a product in a flash of insight.... The truth is, this isn't my experience at all. I've known many people I consider to be creative geniuses, and not just at Pixar and Disney, yet I can't remember a single one who could articulate exactly what this vision was they were striving for when they started.

In my experience, creative people discover and realize their visions over time and through dedicated, protracted struggle. In that way, creativity is more like a marathon than a sprint."

Try not to judge this early work of yours too harshly. There will *always* be more story problems to solve; that is one of a writer's many ongoing jobs. The fact that you've come up against some doesn't mean you have to throw your work out, it just means there's more work to be done.

> *"I started writing songs because I figured if John and Paul could do it, anyone could."*
>
> ~ George Harrison

BELIEVE THAT IT IS POSSIBLE

I may alienate some readers here when I say, for the record, that I think books like *The Secret* are, in a word, horseshit. In my not so humble opinion putting one's wishes out into the universe is not, by itself, going to get anybody to the top of the mountain. If only life, and achieving one's dreams, were so simple.

You can wishful think your life away, but if you're not taking real concrete steps of action toward your goals—and I mean doing serious, consistent, usually hard work—you're probably not going to get very far. Training, preparation, diligence, persistence— these old-fashioned virtues are essential to achieving one's goals. And even if you've done all of this, and you might have the best team, Sherpas, conditioning, etc. in the world, stuff still happens. The weather changes, someone gets sick, other elements out of your control intervene, and you don't get there—this time.

But here's what I do believe: If you don't combine your efforts and hard work with the sincere, heartfelt conviction that your goals are indeed achievable, then you've already lost. If you don't deep down in your heart of hearts allow yourself to believe there's even a slim chance, even an outside, one-in-a-million, why *not* me chance of accomplishing your dream, *and* that you deserve it, then how can you possibly ever hope to make it a reality? You must believe that whatever your goal is, it can be achieved or you will never make the sacrifices or invest the effort necessary to get there.

When I was writing *Only You*, I was unemployed and in debt. (I don't, by the way, recommend this.) Anyway, around that time I read a quote from Paul McCartney who said that people always thought the Beatles were not materialistic and he said nothing could've been further from the truth. They were four working-class lads from Liverpool, they aspired to the good life. He said that as they sat down to write a song, they would say to themselves: "Let's write a house today. Let's write a pool today."

I loved this story. And it inspired me to sit down and write a description of the dream house I wanted, and ultimately wound up being able to buy. But I found this difficult to do at first, I felt like an imposter. And that was when it struck me that if I couldn't manage, in the privacy of my own crappy apartment, to write down on paper what I wanted how could I ever possibly hope to actually make it happen?

Shortly after I sold the *Only You* script, I showed a close friend what I had written and he said, "I'm really glad you didn't show me this before, because it would've seemed kind of pathetic." Understandable, but it turned out not to be pathetic. That vision, the belief in that possibility, however outlandish it may have seemed at the time, helped to keep me going. (Okay, I take back a little of what I said about *The Secret*.)

EMBRACE THE COMPETITION

Much is made in Hollywood of the brutal competition, but competition isn't necessarily a bad thing. It can push us in a healthy way. It's important to remember to rejoice in your friends' successes because, first, life is a lot more fun that way. And second, if your friends are achieving their dreams, it helps to confirm for you that these things are possible. If you are working as hard, or ideally even harder than they are, know that good things are possible for you, too.

Hang around with other writers whose work you admire, who you think are better than you are. Yes, it can sometimes be a little hard on your ego but, as with playing tennis against a better player, it will up your game, and it will help you believe that success is possible for you, too.

TELL YOUR INNER CRITIC TO ZIP IT

Feel free to be outrageous, offensive, bold, bracing, silly, deadly serious, politically incorrect, but most of all *feel free*. Where else can you be so free, if not on the blank page? Write freely, even recklessly, in your first draft. Go ahead and say *anything you want*. How often in life do we get to do that? Just get it down.

I first encountered the importance of shutting up my inner critic when I began working in development as a story editor for Sydney Pollack and my job was to read scripts and write coverage on them. I was so in awe of Sydney and wanted so badly to *impress*, to make every piece of coverage I wrote worthy of publication. As a result, every time at bat I became consumed with thinking I had to be witty and eloquent and profound and brilliant, often about a script that was, alas, none of these things.

I would obsess to the point that I'd find myself utterly tongue—or more accurately, since I was at the keyboard—finger-tied. But I had to produce *something*. I couldn't very well just throw up my hands and claim writer's block, seeing as how he was paying me a weekly salary. When I found myself in such a paralyzed state, often the most freeing thing I could do was to say to myself about a script,"Well, what did you *really* think of it?" I had to try to forget that he was going to read my work, forget about my "performance" and how it might be perceived, and simply get what I thought of the material down on the page in its most uncensored form. And the words would start to flow. And I would clean it up later.

Director Andrew Stanton advises, "Be wrong as fast as you can." In other words, don't agonize, just get *something* down. Then you'll have something to work with.

FEED THE MUSE: MAKE IT YOUR JOB TO STAY INSPIRED

> *"You can't wait for inspiration. You have to go after it with a club."*
>
> ~ Jack London

Diana Vreeland, grand doyenne of fashion and former revered editor of Vogue, has said, "There is only one thing in life, and that's the continual renewal of inspiration." I'm inclined to agree. But inspiration doesn't just happen all of its own accord, and even if it sometimes does, you can't sit around and wait for it. You have to encourage it and, as with so much in life, you must take action and responsibility for making it happen. You must strive to stay connected with that initial spark of creative joy you felt before all those pesky story problems and nasty self-doubts reared their ugly little heads and started dragging your fun, creativity-loving spirit down.

Imagine those Greek Muses are lounging in our heads eating grapes. Those grapes are life, art, music, travel, whatever stirs your passion and inspires you. Make an effort to take these things in as often as possible. Remember, you're not doing this alone. A hungry Muse is a cranky one, a well-fed one is far more likely to show up when you need her.

IF/WHEN YOU FIND YOURSELF STUCK, A FEW MORE SUGGESTIONS TO KEEP YOU GOING:

1. TRUST YOUR INSTINCTS
   Ask yourself, what would *really* happen? Again, sometimes when you're stuck the best strategy is to stop trying to be all clever and brilliant and simply ask yourself, "Well, what would somebody in this situation actually *do*?"

2. GIVE YOURSELF (AND YOUR CHARACTERS) PERMISSION
   To be outrageous. To be brave. To be bold. Otherwise, what really is the point? You may as well sell life insurance.

3. CRANK UP THE MUSIC
   Play soundtracks of movies that are similar in tone and genre to what you're working on, music that inspires in you the emotion you're striving to conjure on the page. It can be surprisingly helpful.

4. SET YOUR INTENTION FOR THE DAY
   Make it five pages or whatever suits your purposes, but create an intention. Otherwise your time will inevitably get eaten up by the minutiae of daily life, (not to mention email and Facebook, Instagram, Twitter or whatever the equivalent of those are in a year or two or three).

5. WRITE WITH CONVICTION

> Have something to say. Be passionate. Jon Favreau, the writer of *Swingers* who's since become a very successful director (*Elf, Iron Man, Chef* and *The Jungle Book* among others) and actor Vince Vaughn wrote an afterword for a published edition of the screenplay for *Swingers* called *The Swingers Rules*. In it, they write, "*The strongest will survives. Don't waste your time filling your head with self-doubt. The competition's fierce, so always give yourself the edge. A sense of self-respect makes all the difference in the world. You can be the king of the jungle or just another hyena cowering at the water hole. It's all up to you.*"

Does this notion of making your work personal and writing from your own passion and conviction seem quaint in the face of things like *X-Men CCLXXXVIII*? Perhaps. But here's the thing: You're never gonna get that gig to write (or rewrite) the sequel to *Spiderman Infinity* until you establish yourself in the business first. And the only way to do that, the only way to break in, short of having a blood relative running a studio, is to create something original that will get you noticed. And where else are you going to find that something but inside yourself?

Your voice, your sensibility, your life experience and perspective on the world is your unique gift and yours alone. Treasure it, but *hone* it. If you truly want to be a writer, then please, I beg of you, don't be a dilettante about it. Take your craft seriously and educate yourself to the best of your ability, so that you can best express what's in your heart and mind and thereby create great movies for the rest of us to enjoy.

If you want to be a screenwriter, know why you're doing it and be willing to suffer the slings and arrows that inevitably come with the territory. Find a support system you can really trust (this is critical) and then take action and keep moving forward. Feed your artistic soul with work that inspires you and keeps you going (this is also critical), and try to keep your eyes focused on the goal and off the obstacles. Commit to working harder than you can possibly imagine, and strive, as Steve Martin advises, to "be so good they can't ignore you."

Finally, remember that ultimately you can't learn how to dance, or how to do much else for that matter, simply by reading about it. It is essential for you to learn the basics of the art form you aspire to create, but then you must get out there and, just as your hero must, take action. You must write. I hope this book has helped encourage you to do that.

> *"Come to the edge."*
>
> *"We might fall!"*
>
> *"Come to the edge."*
>
> *"It's too high!"*
>
> *"Come to the edge."*
>
> *And they came. And he pushed them, and they flew.*
>
> ~ Christopher Logue

I wish you every success, but even more than that, I wish you fulfillment and joy in the process.

ACKNOWLEDGMENTS

I am deeply thankful to the following people for their support, encouragement, assistance and inspiration: Robert Downey Jr., Kathleen Gosnell Seiler, Jennifer Grisanti, Chae Ko, Paula Petrella, Nick Pollack, Jennifer Rima, Al Quattrocchi, Nancy Ross, Jeff Smith, Streetlight Graphics, Joan Sullivan, Linda Venis, Meg Waite Clayton and Julie Walke.

Finally I want to thank my many lovely students and clients who encouraged me to write this book and who have graciously made me feel that my work has enriched their lives.

Made in the USA
San Bernardino, CA
21 March 2020